Best Easy Day Hikes
Vail

Help Us Keep This Guide Up to Date

Every effort has been made by the author and editors to make this guide as accurate and useful as possible. However, many things can change after a guide is published—trails are rerouted, regulations change, facilities come under new management, etc.

We would appreciate hearing from you concerning your experiences with this guide and how you feel it could be improved and kept up to date. While we may not be able to respond to all comments and suggestions, we'll take them to heart and we'll also make certain to share them with the author. Please send your comments and suggestions to the following address:

GPP
Reader Response/Editorial Department
PO Box 480
Guilford, CT 06437

Or you may e-mail us at:

editorial@GlobePequot.com

Thanks for your input, and happy trails!

Best Easy Day Hikes Series

Best Easy Day Hikes
Vail

Maryann Gaug

FALCON GUIDES

GUILFORD, CONNECTICUT
HELENA, MONTANA

AN IMPRINT OF GLOBE PEQUOT PRESS

FALCONGUIDES®

© 2013 Morris Book Publishing, LLC.

FalconGuides is an imprint of Globe Pequot Press.

Falcon and FalconGuides are registered trademarks and Outfit Your Mind is a trademark of Morris Book Publishing, LLC.

Maps created by Alena Joy Pearce and Melissa Baker © Morris Book Publishing, LLC.

Project Editor: David Legere
Layout Artist: Justin Marciano

Library of Congress Cataloging-in-Publication Data is available on file.

ISBN 978-0-7627-8171-3

Printed in the United States of America

10 9 8 7 6 5 4 3 2 1

Contents

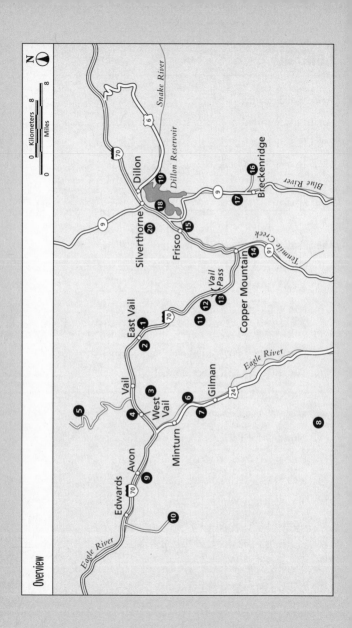

Overview

Acknowledgments

Many thanks to all of my contacts in the USDA Forest Service, Town of Dillon, Town of Breckenridge, Town of Vail, and Town of Avon for working with me on which trails would be most appropriate for this book. Despite the "big brother" image federal and public employees often have, these people love the backcountry and were eager to answer questions, review the chapters, and provide feedback. Thanks to Carol Hunter of Partners for Access to the Woods for the historical background of Julia's Deck and to Jaci Spuhler of Eagle County Library for researching several of my questions.

Because I typically hike the trails by myself, thanks to my good friend Keith Brown, who anxiously awaited my phone calls that I was safe and not lost in the woods.

A special thanks to my mom and my dad, both dead, for encouraging me to do what I want to do and strive for peace and happiness.

Last but not least, thanks to you readers and fellow hikers for buying *Best Easy Day Hikes Vail*. I hope you find it useful and interesting, and may you enjoy many hours hiking the trails described between these covers.

About the Author

Maryann Gaug is an avid hiker and a Master of Leave No Trace as well as a freelance writer and photographer. Her FalconGuides include *Hiking Colorado*, *Best Hikes Near Denver and Boulder*, and *Hiking Colorado's Summit County Area*. A native of Denver, Maryann now lives in Summit County in Silverthorne. For more information check out www.facebook.com/Hiking ColoradoGuides and www.falcon.com/author/maryann-gaug.

Introduction

If you think of world-class skiing and a swank resort for the rich and famous when you hear the word "Vail," the hikes in this book will show you another side to this beautiful section of Colorado. Your first hint is to stand in the middle of Vail Village and look northeast to the craggy 13,000-foot peaks that tower over the Gore Valley. I always imagine myself in Switzerland.

Trails around Vail and neighboring Summit County provide opportunities ranging from a stroll on a paved recreation path to steep ascents accessing waterfalls and lakes to moderate trails wandering through fields of red, white, blue, yellow, and purple wildflowers. The west side of the Gore Range tends to be lusher because storms hit the mountains and drop much of their moisture. Not all the mountains are as steep and craggy as those in the Gore Range. To the west of Vail Pass, the terrain rolls and rises gently to ridges.

The best months for hiking are mid-June through the end of September, but snow may still cover the higher trails until early July. In mid- to late July, make sure to take time to "smell the flowers," for they bloom profusely in the high meadows and along many of the trails. If you're hanging out in the fall (late September), amble along the paths lined with golden aspens. The Vail area boasts vast patches of these deciduous trees. While hiking, feel free to stop, eat lunch, and turn around at any time. The most important thing: Enjoy the beauty of your surroundings at an unhurried pace and a comfortable distance.

As you hike around the beautiful Vail region, capture part of nature's spirit and hold it close to your own. Leave a piece of your spirit as well, so that no matter where you travel or

1

live, the peace and beauty of this wild country will remain with you forever.

High Country Weather

Summers around Vail and Summit County are downright gorgeous. Days start sunny and grow warm (not hot), except for the typical afternoon thunderstorm and a few rainy days during the monsoon in July and August. Evenings turn cool and pleasant after the sun sets. Temperatures typically rise to the seventies and rarely get above eighty-five degrees, while nighttime lows can dip into the low forties. However, a few words of caution are in order. First, at this high elevation skin burns quickly, even on cloudy days. Make sure to apply plenty of sunscreen and apply it often. Second, the weather can change very quickly. Bring an extra layer of clothes for temperature plunges and rain gear for sudden showers. With thunderstorms comes lightning, a killer from above. If you see lightning or hear thunder, head downhill away from high, exposed ridges. Lightning finds the path of least resistance—make sure that path isn't through your body. Third, snow falls, at least a little, pretty much every month of the year up here, including on the Fourth of July.

Critters

The wild animals that you may encounter include pine squirrels, ground squirrels, chipmunks, marmots, pikas, and deer. Black bears (no grizzlies), moose, and mountain lions do live in these parts, so keep your children close to you. If you encounter one of these large animals, do not run. Keep calm and slowly back away. For mountain lions, lift your arms to make yourself look bigger.

Danger from Falling Trees

You're sure to notice dead lodgepole pines along the trails and on hillsides. A drought in the early 2000s weakened the trees enough that they succumbed to mountain bark (pine) beetles. These tiny insects, part of the natural forest cycle, reproduced in epidemic proportions due to the amount of vulnerable trees and successfully attacked healthy trees as well. Very cold winters typically kill many beetles, but recent winters have been relatively mild. Treating the acres of trees involved became impossible. Please be aware that these dead trees can fall at any time, particularly in high winds. Be careful while hiking!

Be Prepared

When choosing a hike, think about your physical condition. Activity is more difficult above 7,000 feet if you're visiting from low elevations. Make sure to eat and drink properly, avoid alcohol for the first few days, and get plenty of rest. For the rockier trails wear good hiking boots to protect your feet. Bring water and snacks with you too. Hiking poles take pressure off your knees and aid your balance. Place your extra clothes, food, water, first-aid kit, whistle, rain gear, camera, appropriate map, binoculars, wet wipes, and *Best Easy Day Hikes Vail* in your day pack. You can rent many items at local outdoor stores. Please note that cell phone service may not be available on the trails.

Leave No Trace

We, as trail users and advocates, must be especially vigilant to make sure our passage leaves no lasting mark. We need to think about thousands of feet instead of just the two we each have. Here are some basic guidelines for preserving trails in the region:

- Be prepared. Bring or wear clothes to protect you from cold, heat, or rain. Use maps to navigate (and do not rely solely on the maps included in this book).

- Avoid damaging trailside soils and plants by remaining on the established route. When the trail is wet, walk through mud puddles to prevent widening the muck.

- Pack out all your own trash, including biodegradable items like orange peels and apple cores. They decay slowly in the dry climate. You might also pack out garbage left by less considerate hikers. Use outhouses at trailheads or along the trail, and keep water sources clean.

- Don't pick wildflowers or gather rocks, antlers, feathers, and other treasures along the trail. Removing these items will only take away from the next hiker's experience.

- Be careful with fire. Use a camp stove for cooking. Be sure it's okay to build a campfire in the area you're visiting—they are prohibited in several locations. Use an existing fire ring, and keep your fire small. Use sticks (no larger than your wrist) from the ground as kindling. Burn all the wood to ash, and be sure the fire is completely out and cold before leaving.

- Don't approach or feed any wild creatures—the ground squirrel eyeing your snack food is best able to survive if it remains self-reliant. Control pets at all times.

- Be kind to other visitors. Be courteous by not making loud noises while hiking, and be aware that you share the trail with others. Yield to other trail users when appropriate.

The "Vail Area" Definition for This Hiking Guide

In less than an hour's drive from Vail, you can reach all the trailheads in this book. In addition to Vail hikes, you can access trails from the nearby towns of Edwards, Avon, and Minturn. Eight trails in Summit County around Dillon, Frisco, Silverthorne, and Breckenridge are also included.

Land Management

The US Department of Agriculture (USDA) Forest Service (the Holy Cross/Eagle Ranger District and the Dillon Ranger District of the White River National Forest) is the contact for most of the trails described in this book. Other agencies involved include the Town of Vail, Town of Avon, Town of Breckenridge, Town of Dillon, Summit County Open Space and Trails, Vail Resorts, and Copper Mountain Resort. Each hike chapter specifies which agency is responsible and how to contact it for more information. Please read trailhead bulletin boards for specific trail rules and regulations. For trails entering the Holy Cross and Eagles Nest Wildernesses, please note that dogs must be on leash and group size is limited to no more than fifteen people. Additional regulations can be found on the websites and bulletin boards.

Public Transportation

Generally speaking, you will need a vehicle to reach the trailheads. If bus service is available, it is noted in the "Finding the trailhead" section.

The Town of Vail has a free bus system. Vail Transportation Center; (970) 479-2178; www.vailgov.com.

Eagle County Regional Transportation (ECO Transit) provides bus service around Eagle County. PO Box 1070, 3289 Cooley Mesa Rd., Gypsum 81637; (970) 328-3520; www.eaglecounty.us/Transit/Contact_Information/.

Summit County has a free bus system called the Summit Stage. PO Box 2179, Frisco 80443; (970) 668-0999; www.summitstage.com.

How to Use This Guide

This guide is designed to be simple and easy to use. Each hike is described with a map and summary information that delivers the trail's vital statistics, including length, difficulty, elevation gain, fees and permits, hours if applicable, canine compatibility, and trail contacts. Directions to the trailhead are also provided, along with a general description of what you'll see along the way. A detailed route finder ("Miles and Directions") sets forth mileages between significant landmarks along the trail. GPS coordinates are WGS84 datum.

Hike Selection

The hikes described in *Best Easy Day Hikes Vail* range from easy to more challenging and sample a variety of different terrain and ecosystems. The hikes range from 0.35 mile to 4.1 miles, with options for shorter excursions. Two hikes require riding a gondola at Vail or a chairlift at Copper Mountain. Three hikes are ADA (Americans with Disabilities Act) accessible, allowing people with disabilities to access view areas or picnic places: Julia's Deck, Osprey Viewpoint, and part of the paved Gore Valley Trail. Four trails lead to relics of the mining era, when gold and silver fever brought people swarming over the hills to make their fortune but often ended up "mining" tourists, harvesting trees, or growing lettuce. The chosen trails wander through wildflower meadows or along cascading creeks, arrive at ridges with stunning views of the Gore Range or Mount of the Holy Cross, or meander through aspen forests.

Difficulty Ratings

As you look around you at the peaks and cliff bands bordering Vail, realize that the terrain tends to go up, and the trails follow. These hikes are all easy, but "easy" is a relative term. Some would argue that no hike involving any kind of climbing is easy, but in the Vail area hills are a fact of life. To aid in the selection of a hike that suits particular needs and abilities, each is rated easy, moderate, or more challenging. Bear in mind that even more challenging routes can be made easy by hiking within your limits and taking rests when you need them.

- Easy hikes are generally short and mostly flat, taking no longer than an hour to complete.

- Moderate hikes involve increased distance and moderate changes in elevation and will take 1 to 2 hours to complete.

- More challenging hikes feature some steep stretches, greater distances, and generally take longer than 2 hours to complete.

These ratings are completely subjective—consider that what you think is easy is entirely dependent on your level of fitness and the adequacy of your gear (primarily shoes). If you are hiking with a group, you should select a hike with a rating that's appropriate for the least fit and prepared in your party.

Approximate hiking times are based on the assumption that on flat ground, most walkers average 2 miles per hour. Adjust that rate by the steepness of the terrain and your level of fitness (subtract time if you're an aerobic animal and add time if you're hiking with kids), and you have a ballpark hiking duration. Be sure to add more time if you plan to picnic or take part in other activities like birding or photography.

Trail Finder

Best Hikes for Geology Lovers
1 Gore Creek Trail
7 Cross Creek Trail
8 Missouri Lakes Trail
12 Shrine Ridge Trail

Best Hikes for Children
2 Gore Valley Trail
4 North Trail
5 Upper Piney River Trail
9 Nottingham Lake
11 Julia's Deck
13 Wilder Gulch Trail
15 Masontown
16 X10U8 and B&B Loop
17 Iowa Hill Trail
18 Osprey Viewpoint
19 Dillon Peninsula
20 Lily Pad Lake Trail

Best Hikes for Great Views
3 Ridge Route
5 Upper Piney River Trail
11 Julia's Deck
12 Shrine Ridge Trail
18 Osprey Viewpoint
19 Dillon Peninsula

Best Hikes for Lake Lovers
20 Lily Pad Lake Trail

Best Hikes for Nature Lovers

1 Gore Creek Trail
3 Ridge Route
5 Upper Piney River Trail
6 Two Elk National Recreation Trail
7 Cross Creek Trail
8 Missouri Lakes Trail
10 East Lake Creek Trail
12 Shrine Ridge Trail
13 Wilder Gulch Trail
14 Hallelujah Self-Guided Nature Trail
18 Osprey Viewpoint
20 Lily Pad Lake Trail

Best Hikes for History Buffs

13 Wilder Gulch Trail
14 Hallelujah Self-Guided Nature Trail
15 Masontown
16 X10U8 and B&B Loop
17 Iowa Hill Trail

Best Hikes in Winter

9 Nottingham Lake
16 X10U8 and B&B Loop
18 Osprey Viewpoint
19 Dillon Peninsula
20 Lily Pad Lake Trail

Map Legend

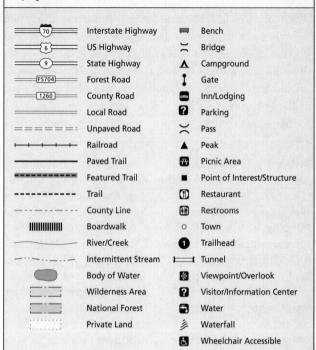

70	Interstate Highway	▭	Bench
6	US Highway	⌣	Bridge
9	State Highway	▲	Campground
FS704	Forest Road	⌶	Gate
1260	County Road	▬	Inn/Lodging
	Local Road	❷	Parking
	Unpaved Road	⌣	Pass
	Railroad	▲	Peak
	Paved Trail	🪧	Picnic Area
	Featured Trail	■	Point of Interest/Structure
	Trail	🍴	Restaurant
	County Line	🍴	Restrooms
	Boardwalk	○	Town
	River/Creek	❶	Trailhead
	Intermittent Stream	⊢⊣	Tunnel
	Body of Water	🔭	Viewpoint/Overlook
	Wilderness Area	❷	Visitor/Information Center
	National Forest	💧	Water
	Private Land	⋙	Waterfall
		♿	Wheelchair Accessible

1 Gore Creek Trail

The Gore Creek Trail climbs steeply at first and then undulates above or along rough-and-tumble Gore Creek. Ascending the drainage, you roam through coniferous forest and open meadows and past aspen trees, lush bushes, and colorful wildflowers—a new scene around each bend. The hike ends at the bridge over Deluge Creek, but you can turn around sooner where there's a nice place to enjoy the cascading creek.

Distance: 3.7 miles out and back, with an option for a shorter hike of 2.0 miles

Hiking time: 1.5 to 2.5 hours

Difficulty: More challenging due to steep spots, rocky terrain, and a 760-foot elevation gain

Trail surface: Dirt with some rocky sections

Best season: June through mid-Oct

Other trail users: Equestrians

Canine compatibility: Dogs must be on leash in the Eagles Nest Wilderness.

Fees and permits: No fee. Limit of fifteen people per group.

Maps: USGS Vail East and Willow Lakes; Nat Geo Trails Illustrated 108 Vail/Frisco/Dillon; Latitude 40° Vail and Eagle Trails; USFS White River National Forest map

Trail contact: USDA Forest Service, Eagle-Holy Cross Ranger District, 24747 US 24, Minturn 81645; (970) 827-5715; www.fs.usda.gov/whiteriver

Special considerations: Hunters may use this area during hunting season. The trail is neither marked nor maintained for winter use. Keep children out of the swiftly flowing creek at all times.

Other: The trail is mainly within the Eagles Nest Wilderness area. Please comply with wilderness regulations.

Finding the trailhead: From I-70 exit 180 (Vail East Entrance), drive on the south side of I-70 on Bighorn Road for 2.1 miles to the trailhead parking (a wide dirt area) on the left side of the road,

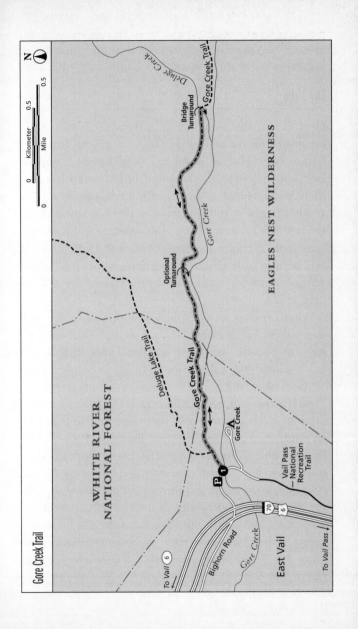

just before Gore Creek Campground. No facilities are located at the trailhead. Bring your own water; the creek is not always near the trail, and creek water should be treated. GPS: N39 37.66' / W106 16.49'

The Hike

Gore Creek, the Gore Range, and various other entities are named for Sir St. George Gore, the Eighth Baronet of Manor Gore. His vast estate was located in northwest Ireland, but he lived south of London. In 1854 the 43-year-old bachelor organized a hunting trip leaving from St. Louis and heading west to New and Old Parks in Colorado and the lower Yellowstone Valley. His entourage and equipment were quite the show. England's most skilled gunsmiths created his gun collection, adorning every square inch of each weapon. Jim Bridger of mountain-man fame became Gore's head guide.

Gore's convoy included forty men plus two valets and a dog handler, one hundred horses, twenty yoke of oxen, fifty hunting hounds, and twenty-eight vehicles, including his fancy yellow-wheeled carriage.

Gore slept and ate in a green-and-white tent with a French carpet laid over a rubber pad. The tent contained a camp stove, chests and trunks, the ornate guns in their racks, an ornamental brass bed, and a fur-lined commode. Servants brought him gourmet-style meals. Every morning Gore's valet would build a fire in the stove and boil water. An hour later Gore took a bath in his oval bathtub, shaved, and then ate breakfast before heading out for the day's adventures.

Indians and whites alike despised Gore for his wanton killing of wildlife. Over three years he reportedly killed more than 2,000 bison, 1,600 elk and deer, and 100 bears, mostly for sport.

The Gore Creek Trail climbs fairly steeply at first but occasionally levels out. Wildflowers bloom in a rainbow of colors. When storms come from the west, they drop more moisture on the west side of the Gore Range, resulting in lush vegetation and many berry bushes. Aspen trees turn golden in the fall, while spruce, fir, and skinny lodgepole pines remain green, or red if bark beetles have killed the tree. The trail wanders high above the creek before meeting it after about 1 mile. Just before Deluge Creek you enter a lush "jungle" and then scramble up a hunk of sloping rock with good places for your feet.

The Gore Creek Trail ends at the top of Red-Buffalo Pass, a ridge that you can see while hiking. From the pass a hiker can either head south to Frisco or continue east to Silverthorne.

Miles and Directions

0.0 Start at the Deluge Lake Trail/Gore Creek Trail bulletin board (elevation: 8,711 feet). Please sign the register a few steps up the trail.

0.1 Arrive at the Deluge Lake Trail junction. Continue straight ahead on the Gore Creek Trail.

0.4 Reach the Eagles Nest Wilderness boundary.

1.0 Arrive at some nice rocks where the creek is close to the trail (GPS: N39 37.80' / W106 15.55'). (**Option:** Turn around here to shorten the hike to 2.0 miles.)

1.2 Continue straight ahead on the main trail past a couple of side trails that head to the right.

1.85 Arrive at Deluge Creek and a nice bridge (GPS: N39 37.74' / W106 14.80'; elevation: 9,480 feet). This area is a good spot for lunch. Return the way you came.

3.7 Arrive back at the trailhead.

2 Gore Valley Trail

Starting by Bighorn Road at Vail's east entrance, this featured section of the paved Gore Valley Trail offers an easy walk along Gore Creek past willows, aspens, lodgepole pines, and grassy meadows. Enjoy the scenery from benches and ADA-accessible picnic tables along the way. Three different turnaround points are suggested.

Distance: 2.7 miles out and back, with options for shorter hikes of 1.3 or 1.6 miles
Hiking time: 30 minutes to 1.8 hours
Difficulty: Easy due to minimal elevation gain; ADA accessible
Trail surface: Paved
Best season: Mid-May through late Oct
Other trail users: Bikers, joggers
Canine compatibility: Dogs must be on leash.

Fees and permits: None
Maps: USGS Vail East; Nat Geo Trails Illustrated 108 Vail/Frisco/Dillon; Latitude 40° Vail and Eagle Trails
Trail contact: Town of Vail, 75 S. Frontage Rd., Vail 81657; (970) 479-2100; www.vailgov.com
Special considerations: Bring water with you, as none is readily available along the trail. The trail is part of Vail Nordic Center in winter, and a pass is required.

Finding the trailhead: From I-70 exit 180 (Vail East Entrance), drive on the south side of I-70 on Bighorn Road to the first left turn, which is trailhead parking. A bus stop is 0.1 mile east on Bighorn Road. Walk across Bighorn Road to the paved recreation path. GPS: N39 38.58' / W106 18.42'

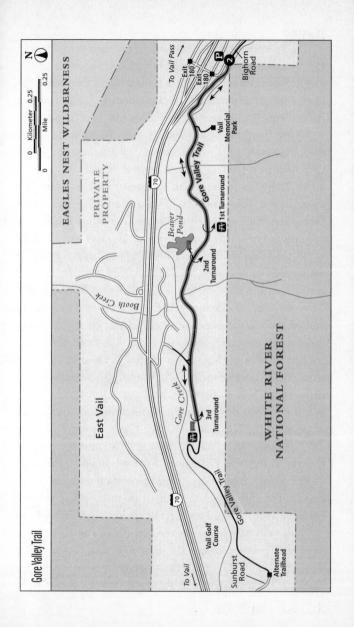

Gore Valley Trail

The Hike

People started homesteading along Gore Creek in around 1884. Besides growing food for their families, they sold lamb, beef, wild game, vegetables, and potatoes to hungry miners. By the early 1900s most of the valley had been settled.

When the Great Depression hit, many homesteaders could no longer hang on to their homes and ranches. The Katsos and Kiahtipes families bought several ranches during the 1930s. These Greek sheepmen obtained permits to graze their sheep in the high meadows of the national forest above the Gore Valley during summers. In winter they moved them west to graze in Utah. Gus Kiahtipes called his ranch the Circle K.

In 1957 Pete Siebert, Earl Eaton, and partners purchased the 500-acre Hanson Ranch, which straddled both sides of US 6 and included parts of the former Circle K and Katsos ranches. They dreamed of developing a European-style ski resort and created the Vail Corporation. Their ski area on the mountain and the village below opened for business in December 1962.

Part of the old Hanson Ranch had been subdivided and planned for development. Not wanting to see every inch of the Gore Valley covered with houses, some Vail citizens talked the town into buying and preserving part of the land as open space. The Katsos Ranch Open Space, created in 1977, goes from the end of Sunburst Drive near the Vail Golf Course to the East Vail exit of I-70. Meanwhile, the Town of Vail had been building a paved recreation trail that would eventually go from Dowd Junction (at the Eagle River) and connect with the Vail Pass Recreation Trail paralleling I-70.

This walk takes you on the section of the Gore Valley Trail that passes through the Katsos Ranch Open Space. The trail crosses Gore Creek on a sturdy wooden bridge. You pass the Vail Memorial Park; a bench sits to the right.

The path wanders farther from I-70, past lodgepole pines, green meadows, and aspen groves that glow gold and orange in fall. The town has placed benches and picnic tables along the way for your enjoyment. The picnic table at 0.65 mile is especially nice, tucked beneath aspen trees. Farther along a beaver lodge sits in a pond. Past here, houses line the north side of Gore Creek.

Enjoy a pleasant walk through this open space area and think back on the history of the area, from the Utes who traveled and hunted here to the homesteaders eking out a living to the amenities of modern Vail.

Miles and Directions

0.0 Start from the edge of Bighorn Road and the short access trail. Head right and then turn right onto the Gore Valley Trail (elevation: 8,370 feet).

0.3 Pass Vail Memorial Park on the left.

0.65 Reach a picnic table on the left among aspen trees, a nice place for an ADA-accessible picnic (GPS: N39 38.66' / W106 19.05'). (**Option:** Return the way you came for a 1.3-mile out-and-back walk.)

0.8 A trail on the right goes to a bench near a beaver pond (not ADA accessible). (**Option:** Return the way you came for a 1.6-mile out-and-back walk.)

1.1 Look across Gore Creek to the log house with a grass roof—a touch of Switzerland.

1.15 Come to milepost 8.5 and a junction with the trail to Booth Creek Park on the right. Continue straight ahead. The trail rises more steeply after here.

1.35 Arrive at a bench and a picnic table on the right (GPS: N39 38.69' / W106 19.78'). Return the way you came for a 2.7-mile out-and-back hike.

2.7 Arrive back at the trailhead.

3 Ridge Route

Ridge Route climbs steadily but easily up a ridge to Wildwood, one of Vail's high points. Along the way you cross several ski runs filled with wildflowers underlining views of Mount of the Holy Cross and Mount Jackson. At Wildwood enjoy the vista of the rugged Gore Range around the building's corner.

Distance: 2.8 miles out and back
Hiking time: 1.5 to 2 hours
Difficulty: Moderate due to a 631-foot elevation gain
Trail surface: Dirt
Best season: Mid-June through Sept (when the Eagle Bahn Gondola is running)
Other trail users: None
Canine compatibility: Dogs are not allowed on the gondola.
Fees and permits: Gondola ticket required to ride gondola to trailhead
Schedule: Check gondola hours at www.vail.com, or call (970) 754-8245.
Maps: USGS Minturn and Red Cliff; Nat Geo Trails Illustrated 108 Vail/Frisco/Dillon; Latitude 40° Vail and Eagle Trails; Vail Summer Activity and Trail Guide
Trail contacts: Vail Mountain Information Center; (970) 754-8245; www.vail.com
USDA Forest Service, Eagle–Holy Cross Ranger District, 24747 US 24, Minturn 81645; (970) 827-5715; www.fs.usda.gov/whiteriver
Special considerations: Bring water, as none is available along the trail. Stay aware of the weather, and be off Ridge Route before thunderstorms start.
Other: Restrooms and restaurants are available in Eagle's Nest at the top of the gondola. Picnic tables and restrooms are available at Wildwood.

Finding the trailhead: From I-70 exit 176 (Vail), on the south side of I-70, turn right where the sign points to Lionshead Parking. Drive 0.3 mile to the visitor parking and park. Restrooms are available on the upper level. At the southwest corner of the parking garage, walk

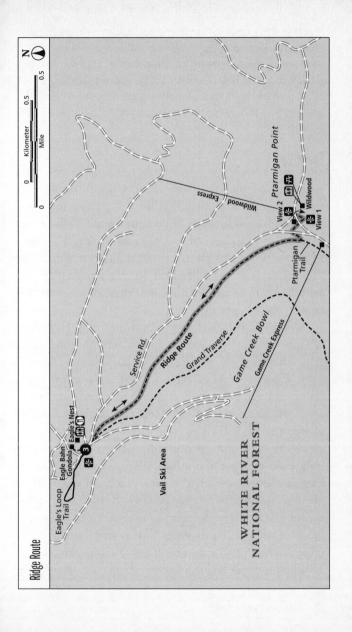

Ridge Route

White River National Forest

Eagle's Loop Trail
Eagle Bahn Gondola
Eagle's Nest
Vail Ski Area
Service Rd
Ridge Route
Grand Traverse
Game Creek Bowl
Game Creek Express
Ptarmigan Trail
View 1
View 2
Wildwood
Ptarmigan Point
Wildwood Express

N

0   0.5   Kilometer
0   0.5   Mile

down the stairs, cross the street, and head under the Eagle Bahn Shops arch. Turn left at the Arabelle arch. Walk down the path and you'll see the gondola ahead. The ticket office is to the left. Ride the gondola to Eagle's Nest. When you exit the gondola, turn right on the paved path and head toward the observation deck. The Ridge Route Trailhead is at the edge of the paved path and dirt. GPS: N39 37.06' / W106 23.19'

The Hike

Humans have used the Gore Creek valley for many years. Campsite remains unearthed at the rest area on the top of Vail Pass date back about 7,000 years. In the 1860s miners swarmed to today's Summit County and Leadville in search of riches. When the great fortunes didn't materialize, they decided to homestead the land, settling around the place we call Vail. They raised animals and vegetables to feed their families and hungry miners.

World War II brought young men to Camp Hale, south of Gore Creek, to train in the Army's 10th Mountain Division. After the war ended, one of the veterans, Peter W. Seibert, became a ski instructor at Aspen and later managed Loveland Basin Ski Area. A friend, Earl Eaton, had "discovered" the south side of Vail Mountain while looking for uranium in 1954. The two men skied the mountain, finding plenty of snow and great powder. Seibert envisioned not only a ski area but also a base village, similar to those in Europe. Seibert and his company purchased the 500-acre Hanson Ranch, which straddled US 6. In 1959 they applied to the USDA Forest Service for the permit to build their dream. They enticed investors and secured loans for their project. The Vail Corporation began clearing ski runs and installing a gondola and chairlifts on the mountain while building shops, restaurants, and hotels in the valley. Interested homeowners purchased 121 residential lots.

The ski area opened in December 1962 with a dearth of snow, but the white gold fell by Christmas. Vail has evolved into a world-renowned destination. If you have time, visit the Colorado Ski & Snowboard Museum and Hall of Fame for more history of the sport.

Wildflowers lining the trail include blue lupines, red and rosy paintbrush, white yarrow with its feathery leaves, and blue bell-shaped harebells. On the way down the view includes parts of Avon, Edwards to the west, and the Flat Tops to the northwest.

Miles and Directions

0.0 Start at the edge of the paved trail and dirt (elevation: 10,350 feet). You'll see a sign for Ridge Route, a singletrack trail a little to the left. Do not hike up the road.

0.04 Arrive at the junction of Ridge Route and Grand Traverse. Turn left onto Ridge Route.

0.25 Cross a faded road and head straight ahead.

1.2 Come to the junction of Ridge Route and Ptarmigan. Turn left to continue to Wildwood.

1.4 Arrive at the Wildwood building and the tops of Wildwood Express and Game Creek Express lifts. Walk to the northwest corner of the building for a great view of the Gore Range (GPS: N39 36.35' / W106 22.18'; elevation: 10,982 feet). Return the way you came.

2.8 Arrive back at Eagle's Nest.

4 North Trail

This pleasant hike takes you through various types of vegetation to sparkly little Buffehr Creek. You first pass aspen trees with pink Woods' rose underneath. The trail then crosses an open grassy area with a great view of unnamed pointy peaks in the Gore Range to the east (right). A big log provides a nice viewpoint up Buffehr Creek before the trail descends through thick thimbleberry bushes to the creek below.

Distance: 2.0 miles out and back

Hiking time: 1 to 1.5 hours

Difficulty: Moderate due to a 280-foot elevation gain

Trail surface: Dirt

Best season: June 15 through Oct

Other trail users: Mountain bikers, equestrians

Canine compatibility: Dogs must be on leash.

Fees and permits: None

Schedule: North Trail is closed Apr 15 to June 15 for elk calving season.

Maps: USGS Vail West; Nat Geo Trails Illustrated 108 Vail/Frisco/Dillon; Latitude 40° Vail and Eagle Valley Trails; USFS White River National Forest map

Trail contacts: USDA Forest Service, Eagle–Holy Cross Ranger District, 24747 US 24, Minturn 81645; (970) 827-5715; www.fs.usda.gov/whiteriver

Special considerations: Watch for mountain bikers, especially on the North Trail where it narrows as it passes through a thick patch of thimbleberry bushes. Bring water, or be prepared to treat creek water.

Finding the trailhead: From I-70 exit 173 (West Vail), drive east on the North Frontage Road past Safeway, City Market, and other stores and restaurants. At 0.6 mile by the mile marker 174 sign, turn left onto Buffehr Creek Road. Drive 0.25 mile to the trailhead and parking area on the left. No facilities are available. Cross the bridge

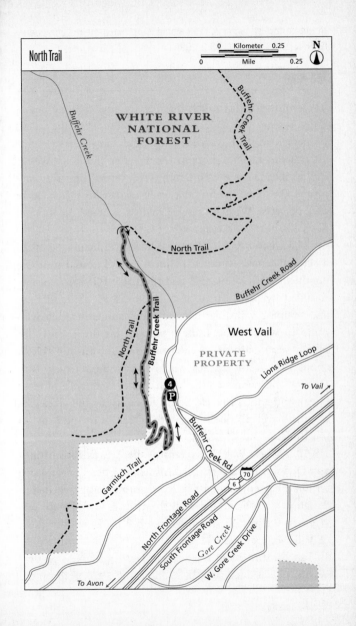

at the northwest corner of the parking lot to reach the bulletin board.
GPS: N39 38.22' / W106 24.93'

The Hike

Try to imagine the trailhead as part of a ranch, long before
the town of Vail and the ski area existed. By the 1880s
homesteaders had wandered into the Gore Creek valley,
establishing ranches, hoping for a better life. John Wesley
Phillips headed one such family. With several mines around
nearby Red Cliff, he found a ready market for spring lambs
and potatoes. With fourteen children to feed, he hunted
deer, elk, bear, grouse, and rabbit.

The Denver & Rio Grande (D&RG) railroad established
a station named Minturn in June 1887. Located near the
confluence of Gore Creek and the Eagle River, it was sur-
rounded by many farms and ranches. With a roundhouse
and shipping yards, the railroad hired numerous men who
came to work. Jacob Buffehr worked for the D&RG for
fifteen years and was an alderman in Minturn in 1911. In
about 1916 Jacob and his wife, Mary, decided to try dairy
farming and purchased the ranch at the confluence of Gore
Creek and another creek. Some accounts say the creek was
originally called Willow; today the creek bears the name of
the Buffehr family.

After World War II, veterans of the Army's 10th Mountain Division realized that Vail Mountain offered ideal skiing
terrain. They envisioned a ski community and proceeded to
design it and obtain approvals from the USDA Forest Service. Vail ski area opened in December 1962, and the Town
of Vail incorporated in 1966.

Fast forward about thirty years. The Eagles Nest Wilderness had been designated by Congress in 1976. Trails in the

area are fairly steep and are open only to foot travel and equestrians. With mountain biking a fast-growing sport and some existing trails and roads contouring along the hills above town to the north, the idea grew to develop a trail system from West Vail to East Vail. Hikers could also access it from their neighborhoods for easier walks than the wilderness area offered. In 1996 the Town of Vail partnered with the USDA Forest Service to design and build new tread and to improve existing trails. The town funded the construction, including a forest service trail crew. Volunteers for Outdoor Colorado built one section of tread. The trail from Arosa Drive in West Vail to Son of Middle Creek Trailhead near East Vail was completed in 1999.

Enjoy this little hike up into the hills on the north side of Vail to a sparkling little creek.

Miles and Directions

0.0   Start at the North Trail System bulletin board (elevation: 8,160 feet). You're on the Buffehr Creek Trail.

0.2   Arrive at the junction with the Garmisch Trail, which comes in from the left. Turn right and head uphill.

0.75 Arrive at the junction with the North Trail. Continue basically straight ahead on the North Trail (elevation: 8,440 feet).

0.85 Reach a flat view spot with a big log to sit on to your right.

1.0   Come to Buffehr Creek crossing (GPS: N39 38.57' / W106 25.07'; elevation: 8,400 feet). Enjoy some time on either side of the creek. Return the way you came.

2.0   Arrive back at the trailhead.

5 Upper Piney River Trail

The Piney River, fed by snow that cloaks the spectacular peaks of the Gore Range, flows through a beautiful valley edged by aspen on the north and spruce and fir on the south. The first 1.3 miles of the Upper Piney River Trail undulates gently through meadows with good spots for lunch, relaxation, and great views.

Distance: 2.6 miles out and back, with an option to extend the hike to 6.0 miles
Hiking time: 1 to 1.75 hours
Difficulty: Easy due to an 80-foot elevation gain
Trail surface: Dirt
Best season: June through Oct
Other trail users: Equestrians
Canine compatibility: Dogs must be on leash in the Eagles Nest Wilderness.
Fees and permits: No fee. Limit of fifteen people per group.
Maps: USGS Vail East and Vail West; Nat Geo Trails Illustrated 108 Vail/Frisco/Dillon; Latitude 40° Summit County Trails; USFS White River National Forest map
Trail contact: USDA Forest Service, Eagle–Holy Cross Ranger District, 24747 US 24, Minturn

81645; (970) 827-5715; www.fs.usda.gov/whiteriver
Special considerations: Hunters use this area during hunting season. The road is closed for the winter 10.5 miles from the trailhead—snowmobiles, cross-country skiers, and snowshoers recreate on the Red Sandstone Road.
Other: Bring water because the creek is far from the trail along this hike. Until you reach the Wilderness boundary, the trail passes through the private Piney River Ranch on an easement. Please stay on the trail. The ranch offers accommodations and camping: www.pineyriverranch.com. The trail is mainly within the Eagles Nest Wilderness area. Please comply with wilderness regulations.

Finding the trailhead: From I-70 exit 176 (Vail), turn north to the North Frontage Road and turn left. Continue 3 miles to Red Sandstone Road and turn right. At the third switchback at 0.7 mile, head a

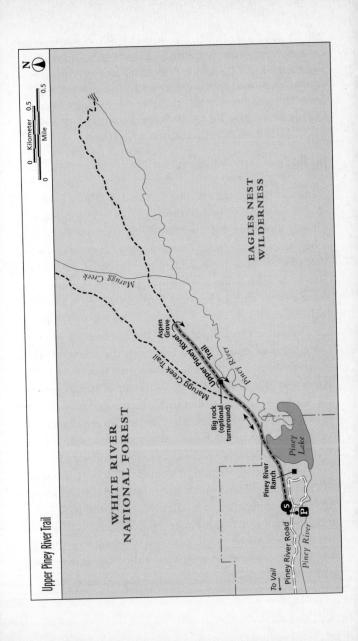

Upper Piney River Trail

little left onto the dirt Red Sandstone Road, FDR 700. Passenger cars can easily navigate the road, although it can be quite bumpy with washboards. Follow the signs to Piney River Ranch and Piney Lake. From where the road turns to dirt, it's a 10.5-mile drive to the trail-head. The parking lot is on the right before the ranch gate. No public facilities are available. The trail starts across the road. GPS: N39 43.24' / W106 24.30' at the trailhead bulletin board.

The Hike

Frank and Al Marugg first homesteaded the Piney Lake area. At the time, early 1900s, silver fox furs sold for a decent amount of money, and the brothers started a fox farm. Avid fishermen, they also built a summer resort at the lake. By the 1930s brook trout were stocked in the lake and it became a favorite fishing place of people living in Minturn and along Gore Creek (where Vail is today). Access was mainly by horse.

Over time the Denver Water Board obtained property along the west end of Piney Lake with the intent to divert water through a tunnel under the Gore Range to Dillon Reservoir. Water from Dillon Reservoir is transported via the Roberts Tunnel to the South Platte River to Denver. The project never happened, but Denver Water still owns the land. Piney River Ranch has a long-term lease with Denver Water to use the area where its buildings are located.

The trail contours along a sloping meadow to the north of the ranch buildings and lake, beneath red cliffs and aspen groves. An abundance of wildflowers grace the trail. At 0.5 mile the trail enters the Eagles Nest Wilderness. Congress officially designated the Eagles Nest Wilderness on July 12, 1976, after negotiations settled the many battles over water and a route for I-70.

The Piney River lazily snakes its way through willows and meadows south of the trail. Just past the junction with the Marugg Creek Trail, a large rock slab on the right is a nice place to enjoy the view. At 1.3 miles a spur trail leads to a grove of aspen trees and some nice rocks. This spot is the turnaround for this hike.

As an alternative, you can continue on the Upper Piney Trail another 1.7 miles to Upper Piney Falls. The route becomes more challenging as it switchbacks up a hillside, crosses numerous little creeks, and then drops down through a rocky area to the river. The falls are to the right where the river descends through big rock slabs. Beyond the turnaround at 1.3 miles, the trail gains 340 feet and then descends 280 feet to the falls.

Miles and Directions

0.0 Start at the Upper Piney Trail bulletin board to the north of the parking lot (elevation: 9,360 feet). The trail heads right along the north shore of Piney Lake.

0.5 Reach the Eagles Nest Wilderness boundary.

0.7 Arrive at the junction with the Marugg Creek Trail. Continue straight ahead.

0.8 Look for a side trail heading to the right to a big rock slab. You can enjoy the view from the rock and return the way you came or continue another 0.5 mile.

1.3 Look for a side trail heading to the right to a slab of rock by some aspen trees (GPS: N39 43.80' / W106 23.09'; elevation: 9,400 feet). The rock slab is a great place for lunch and relaxing. Return the way you came. (**Option:** Follow the Upper Piney Trail another 1.7 miles to Upper Piney Falls. This extension increases the out-and-back hike to 6.0 miles.)

2.6 Arrive back at the trailhead.

6 Two Elk National Recreation Trail

Two Elk National Recreation Trail crosses a ridge over Two Elk Pass between Minturn and I-70 near East Vail. This hike explores only a small part of the trail on the west side, a pleasant journey through thick forest, past rocky outcrops, and among fields of colorful wildflowers. The first part of the trail is gentle and then climbs gradually, great for a fun family hike. Three turnaround options are provided.

Distance: 1.6 miles out and back, with options to extend the hike to 2.4 or 5.8 miles
Hiking time: 1 to 1.5 hours
Difficulty: Moderate due to a 250-foot elevation gain
Trail surface: Dirt
Best season: July through mid-Oct
Other trail users: Mountain bikers, equestrians
Canine compatibility: Dogs must be under voice control.
Fees and permits: None
Schedule: The trail after the first 2 miles is closed May 6 to July 1 for elk calving (across Vail's Back Bowls). The access road is closed 1.3 miles from the trailhead from Dec 1 to Apr 14.
Maps: USGS Minturn and Red Cliff; Nat Geo Trails Illustrated 108 Vail/Frisco/Dillon; Latitude 40° Vail and Eagle Trails; USFS White River National Forest map
Trail contact: USDA Forest Service, Eagle–Holy Cross Ranger District, 24747 US 24, Minturn 81645; (970) 827-5715; www.fs .usda.gov/whiteriver
Special considerations: Numerous berry bushes line the trail at the west end. Be bear aware, especially in late August and September as bears fatten up for the winter. Hunters may use this area during hunting season. The trail is neither marked nor maintained for winter use. Bring your own water; the creek is not always near the trail, and creek water should be treated.

Two Elk National Recreation Trail

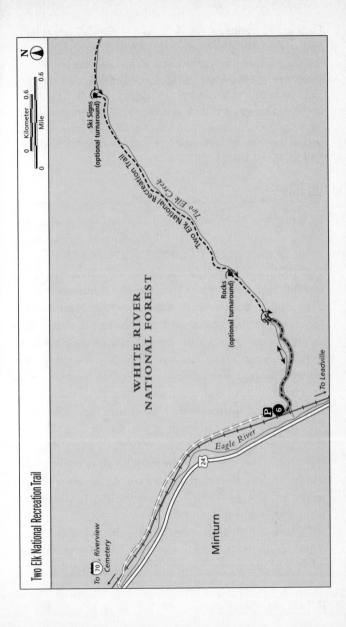

White River National Forest

Minturn

To 70, Riverview Cemetery

Eagle River

24

To Leadville

Two Elk National Recreation Trail

Two Elk Creek

Rocks (optional turnaround)

Ski Signs (optional turnaround)

P
6

N

0   0.6
Kilometer

0   0.6
Mile

Finding the trailhead: From I-70 exit 171 (West US 6/East US 24 Minturn/Leadville), drive south on US 24 through Minturn 2.5 miles to Cemetery Road. Turn left; then stay left and cross the railroad tracks. Turn right at the next intersection and drive past the cemetery. Turn right at the Y to Two Elk Trail and shooting range. The road gets narrow and bumpy here. At the next Y turn left. Drive past the shooting range. The total mileage from US 24 is 1.8 miles. The road dead-ends at the trailhead. No facilities are available at the trailhead. GPS: N39 33.95' / W106 24.07'

The Hike

In September 1979 the White River National Forest submitted an application to the US secretary of agriculture to designate the Two Elk Trail #2005 as a National Recreation Trail (NRT). Congress passed the National Trail System Act in 1968, which recognizes special trails in different regions. They can be designated as National Scenic, National Historic, or National Recreation Trails. The first two require an act of Congress, but either the secretary of the interior or secretary of agriculture can approve NRTs. The agency that manages the trail must submit an application for designation.

The Two Elk Trail application noted the closeness to I-70, Vail, the metropolitan Denver area, and Glenwood Springs. The scenic views from the top of Two Elk Pass were described, including Mount of the Holy Cross. The trail crosses the bottom of the back bowls of Vail ski area: Sundown, Sunup, Teacup, and China. These areas provide wildlife habitat for deer, elk, chipmunks, gray jays, snowshoe hares, and other small wildlife.

When you enter the forest around mile 0.2, look around at the various bushes and flowers. The bushes with the large leaves and big white flowers or large raspberry-like fruits are thimbleberries. Humans have used the thimbleberry for both food and medicinal purposes. The pretty pink flower with five large petals is the Woods' rose, commonly found in aspen forests and along trails. Another bush flourishing in moister areas along the trail is twinberry honeysuckle. Two yellow flowers bloom in pairs, and when the purple fruits ripen, the "twin" aspect is very obvious. Other flowers you'll see include yellow paintbrush and blue harebells (think bluebells).

The trail travels high above the creek to the bridge. Creekside vegetation is fairly thick, containing many bushes and cottonwood trees. To the south of the trail, conifer trees cover the hillside with occasional aspen. The featured hike ends at the bridge over Two Elk Creek, but you can continue to explore this beautiful little area for as long as you feel like hiking.

Miles and Directions

0.0 Start at the Two Elk Trailhead bulletin board (elevation: 8,030 feet). At the first Y in the trail, go right and cross a bridge. At the next Y turn left and head upstream.

0.2 Pass a cairn supporting a post that says Two Elk Trail.

0.8 Arrive at the bridge over Two Elk Creek (GPS: N39 34.02' / W106 23.40'; elevation: 8,280 feet). Return the way you came. (**Option:** For a longer hike, 2.4 miles out and back, continue to mile 1.2, where a rock band borders the trail on the left side and the creek is close on the right. GPS: N39 34.23' / W106 23.07'. Or, for a 5.8-mile trek, continue to mile 2.9, where you'll see a big ski area directional sign on the left after you cross a little creek. GPS: N39 35.03' / W106 21.75'; elevation: 9,040 feet. The meadow is a nice place for lunch.)

1.6 Arrive back at the trailhead.

7 Cross Creek Trail

Hike along an undulating, rocky trail through a forest lush with wildflowers and berry bushes. Spruce, fir, lodgepole pine, and aspen grow amid house-sized boulders draped in moss and lichen. Cross Creek tumbles where the land drops steeply and slows into pools where fish tease anglers.

Distance: 2.5 miles out and back

Hiking time: 1 to 2 hours

Difficulty: Moderate due to a 280-foot elevation gain

Trail surface: Rocky dirt trail

Best season: Late June through Sept

Other trail users: Equestrians

Canine compatibility: Dogs must be on leash.

Fees and permits: No fee. Each party must have one free self-issued Wilderness Use Permit. Limit of fifteen people per group.

Maps: USGS Minturn; Nat Geo Trails Illustrated 108 Vail/Frisco/Dillon; Latitude 40° Vail and Eagle Trails; USFS White River National Forest map

Trail contact: USDA Forest Service, Eagle–Holy Cross Ranger District, 24747 US 24, Minturn 81645; (970) 827-5715; www.fs.usda.gov/whiteriver

Special considerations: Hunters may use this area during hunting season. Bring water with you, as the trail is not always near the creek. Remember to treat any water that you obtain from Cross Creek. The access road is closed from early November until June 20.

Other: The trail is mainly within the Holy Cross Wilderness. Please comply with wilderness regulations.

Finding the trailhead: From I-70 exit 171 (West US 6/East US 24 Minturn/Leadville), drive south on US 24 through Minturn for 4.9 miles to Tigiwon Road/FR 707 (just past mile marker 148). Turn right and drive 1.7 miles to the Cross Creek Trailhead on the right side of the road. Parking is available on the left as well. No facilities are

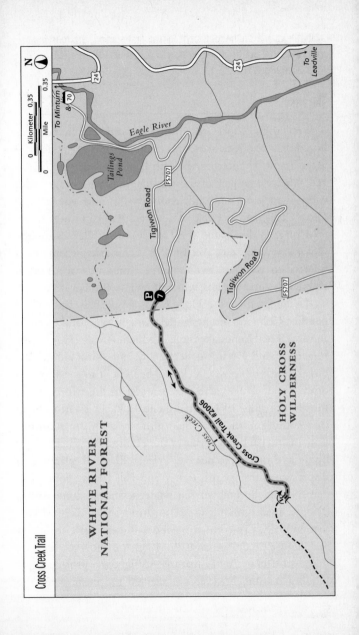

Cross Creek Trail

available at the trailhead. Except for the first section, the road is narrow. Please fill out the free self-issued Wilderness Use Permit. GPS: N39 32.93' / W106 25.11'

The Hike

The trail to the Cross Creek bridge takes you past humongous boulders, across rock slabs, and through a mixed conifer and aspen forest. Thimbleberries, with huge raspberry-like leaves and flowers, line part of the way. The scenery changes with every twist, turn, and undulation. By 0.9 mile you can see Cross Creek, and a couple of side trails lead you to the creek.

Congress designated the Holy Cross Wilderness in the Colorado Wilderness Act of 1980. The area is sometimes referred to as a water wilderness; melting snow feeds many alpine lakes and streams, which flow into the Eagle River.

Designation of the Holy Cross Wilderness was full of conflict. Colorado Springs and Aurora owned water rights in the area. The Homestake Project, which includes Homestake Reservoir and a water-collection system along Homestake Creek south of Cross Creek, had been built in the 1960s to divert about 27,000 acre-feet of water to the two cities on the eastern slope of Colorado. The 1980 act even specified that nothing in the act would interfere with the construction, maintenance, or repair of the Homestake Water Development Project. Homestake Project Phase II planned to divert water from Cross Creek and Fall Creek. Four small dams would be built in the wilderness area, along with a 13-mile underground tunnel to divert about 22,000 acre-feet annually. Concerns arose about the extensive meadows and high-altitude wetlands. In 1982 the Holy Cross Wilderness Defense Fund organized to fight the project. Eagle County became involved and denied the permits for the project. Lawsuits were filed, won, lost, and overturned for several years. In 1994 the Colorado Court of Appeals upheld Eagle County's decision to deny the construction permits for Homestake II. Both the Colorado Supreme Court and the US Supreme Court declined to hear the case.

Take some time to enjoy Cross Creek, where fish cavort in the broad flat stretches. In other places the creek tumbles in cascades and little falls as the land drops steeply.

Miles and Directions

0.0 Start at the Cross Creek Trail bulletin board (elevation: 8,514 feet). The wilderness boundary sign is 150 feet ahead.

0.1 Pass a flat slab of rock. The trail drops about 80 feet, only to start climbing again.

0.8 Arrive at a big mossy rock wall on the left and a trail that descends to the creek on the right. Some flat rocks and a nice cascade make this side trip worthwhile (it's about 320 feet out and back).

0.9 After crossing a flat rock slab, look to your right for a trail (GPS: N39 32.63' / W106 25.86') heading toward the creek (about 160 feet out and back). Flat rocks next to the creek make a great lunch spot. Fish jump and swim in the quiet pools.

1.25 Arrive at the bridge over Cross Creek (GPS: N39 32.45' / W106 26.03'; elevation: 8,720 feet). Some lunch spots are available on the other side of the bridge. Return the way you came.

2.5 Arrive back at the trailhead.

8 Missouri Lakes Trail

The beautiful Missouri Lakes Trail wanders through forest, over some slabs of rocks, across crystal-clear streams, along meadows of colorful wildflowers, past waterfalls, and near some interesting mini-canyons. This chapter describes the trail to three turnaround points (easy to more challenging) because the hike to the lakes is very challenging. This trail provides something for everyone in a magnificent part of Eagle County.

Distance: 3.0 miles out and back, with options to shorten the hike to 1.7 or 2.6 miles
Hiking time: 1.5 to 2.5 hours
Difficulty: More challenging due to a 790-foot elevation gain
Trail surface: Dirt and rock slabs
Best season: July through Sept
Other trail users: Equestrians
Canine compatibility: Dogs must be on leash in the Holy Cross Wilderness.
Fees and permits: No fee. Each party must have one free self-issued Wilderness Use Permit. Limit of fifteen people per group.
Maps: USGS Mount of the Holy Cross and Mount Jackson; Nat Geo Trails Illustrated 126 Holy Cross/Ruedi Reservoir; Latitude

40° Vail and Eagle Trails; USFS White River National Forest map
Trail contact: USDA Forest Service, Eagle-Holy Cross Ranger District, 24747 US 24, Minturn 81645; (970) 827-5715; www.fs .usda.gov/whiteriver
Special considerations: Hunters may use this area during hunting season. Bring your own water; the creek is not always near the trail, and creek water should be treated. FR 703/Homestake Road is closed by snow during winter—ski or snowshoe!
Other: Most of this trail is in the Holy Cross Wilderness. Please comply with wilderness regulations. Campfires are not permitted within the Missouri Creek drainage or near Missouri Lakes.

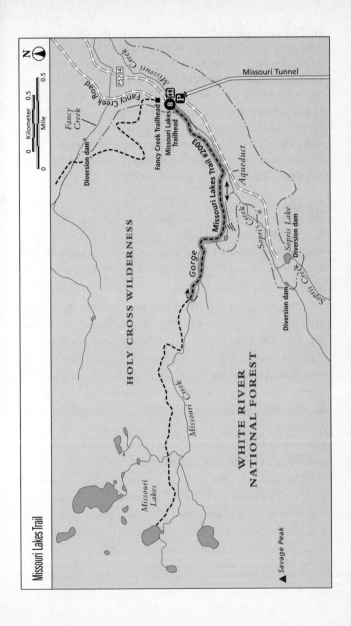

Missouri Lakes Trail

Finding the trailhead: From I-70 exit 171 (West US 6/East US 24 Minturn/Leadville), drive south on US 24 through Minturn for 12.9 miles to FR 703/Homestake Road, just past mile marker 156. Make a sharp right turn onto FR 703, which is dirt and narrow in spots. The road can be rough with washboards but is passable by passenger cars. At 7.8 miles the road reaches a Y intersection. Turn right here onto the road to Missouri Creek Trail (FR 704) and drive 2.2 miles to the trailhead parking lot for both Missouri Lakes and Fancy Pass. Missouri Lakes Trail is to the left. A vault toilet is available; bring your own water. GPS: N39 23.40' / W106 28.25'

The Hike

Part of this hike lies within the Holy Cross Wilderness, which was designated by Congress in the Colorado Wilderness Act of 1980. Its many alpine lakes and streams form the headwaters of the Eagle River.

At mile 0.9 of this hike, you pass a diversion dam and little pond just before the Holy Cross Wilderness boundary sign. The dam is part of the Homestake Project, which includes Homestake Reservoir and a water-collection system along Homestake Creek. Built in the 1960s, the project diverts about 27,000 acre-feet of water to Colorado Springs and Aurora, eastern-slope cities that own the water rights. Water is more abundant on the less-populated western slope than the drier, heavily populated eastern slope, and diverting water from west to east started in the late 1800s.

The first 0.5 mile is quite gentle; the trail then climbs past a nice waterfall dropping down rocky ledges. Beyond the wilderness boundary sign, the trail climbs more steeply, sometimes crossing over big slabs of rock. Notice the white veins and swirls of quartz running through the rocks. You'll cross Missouri Creek on a bridge at a cool little gorge. At

1.5 miles the creek flows through a meadow with jagged peaks in the distance.

Miles and Directions

0.0 Start at the Missouri Lakes Trailhead bulletin board (elevation: 10,010 feet).

0.85 Enjoy the waterfall to the left of the trail. (**Option:** For a short, easy hike, turn around here. The trail to this point is fairly gentle, passing through lodgepole pine and spruce and fir forest. Strawberries, raspberries, geraniums, cinquefoil, pearly everlasting, and other wonderful wildflowers line the path.)

0.9 Arrive at a diversion dam and the Holy Cross Wilderness boundary. The trail starts to climb more steeply and sometimes up rock slabs.

1.3 Cross a bridge over Missouri Creek by a narrow little gorge (GPS: N39 23.27' / W106 29.34'; elevation: 10,680 feet). (**Option:** For a more challenging hike, turn around here. The scenery and little gorge are worth the extra effort.)

1.5 The creek is close to the trail with some nice views of peaks ahead (GPS: N39 23.33' / W106 29.47'; elevation: 10,800 feet). Return the way you came.

3.0 Arrive back at the trailhead.

9 Nottingham Lake

Take an easy stroll around Nottingham Lake in the middle of Avon. A kids' playground, picnic tables, fishing pier, and nice views over the lake to Beaver Creek ski area reward you on your walk.

Distance: 0.8-mile loop
Hiking time: 20 to 45 minutes
Difficulty: Easy; ADA accessible with less than a 30-foot elevation gain
Trail surface: Paved
Best season: Apr through Oct
Other trail users: Joggers, bicyclists
Canine compatibility: Dogs must be on leash.
Fees and permits: None unless group is larger than fifty people

Schedule: Sunrise to 10 p.m. daily
Maps: USGS Edwards; Nat Geo Trails Illustrated 121 Eagle/Avon; Latitude 40° Vail and Eagle Trails
Trail contact: Town of Avon, 1 Lake St., Avon 81620; (970) 748-4000; www.avon.org
Special considerations: Swimming, wading, or playing is prohibited in Nottingham Lake because it is a backup water supply for Avon.

Finding the trailhead: From I-70 exit 167 (Avon), head south toward town, and be careful at each roundabout. In 0.2 mile turn right onto Benchmark Road (sign for Avon Municipal Court Complex). Drive 0.4 mile into the parking lot by the police station and town hall. Restrooms and water are located in the town hall during business hours. The trailhead is in the northwest corner of the parking lot by the log cabin. GPS: N39 38.17' / W106 31.75'

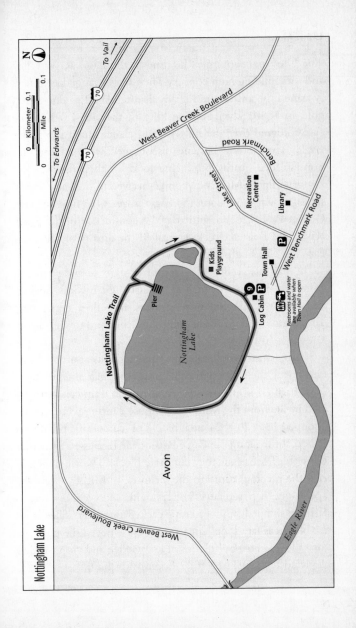

Nottingham Lake

To Vail

To Edwards

West Beaver Creek Boulevard

Benchmark Road

Lake Street

Recreation Center

Library

West Benchmark Road

Kids Playground

Town Hall

Log Cabin

Restrooms and water are available when Town Hall is open

Nottingham Lake Trail

Pier

Nottingham Lake

Avon

West Beaver Creek Boulevard

Eagle River

N

0   Kilometer   0.1

0   Mile   0.1

The Hike

The Utes spent summers hunting in the Eagle River Valley and surrounding high country. Their lives changed as miners swarmed the area around Leadville after Abe Lee discovered gold in 1860. Silver became king in the late 1870s. Miners wandered over the hills, staking claims along the upper Eagle River. Some became discouraged with mining and homesteaded nearby, producing food for their families and hungry miners. More newcomers arrived in the early 1880s, setting down roots along the Eagle River. One homesteader, George A. Townsend, settled at the confluence of the Eagle River and Beaver Creek. He called the area Avondale, perhaps after an English town.

In the late 1880s the Denver & Rio Grande railroad extended its line from Leadville to Glenwood Springs and on to the Aspen mining areas. It built a depot near Townsend's land. At some point the depot and town became known as just Avon.

Farmers grew hay, potatoes, peas, and oats and raised cattle. During the 1920s lettuce became a popular and profitable crop. Farmers shipped their crispy crop in train cars refrigerated by ice from the Minturn icehouse. During winter, crews chopped 18 × 20 × 24-inch blocks of ice out of a pond near Pando, south along the Eagle River near Tennessee Pass. After the water froze again, they cut more blocks. The ice train carried the precious cargo to the icehouse in Minturn for storage. Modern refrigerated railcars didn't exist at the time, so farmers shipped summer crops packed in railcars filled with ice blocks as far as the East Coast. Deer enjoyed the tasty lettuce too. Eventually, lack of soil knowledge and crop rotation depleted the soil. The lettuce boom went bust.

In 1887 William and Angeline Nottingham homesteaded at Avon, eventually enlarging their property with six more homesteads. Their profitable operation included part of today's Avon, the Beaver Creek valley, and the upper portion of Bachelor Gulch. Their three sons inherited different sections of the ranch. By 1972 times had changed, and grandson Willis sold his ranch to Vail Associates to become Beaver Creek resort. Harry Nottingham sold his land along the Eagle River to Benchmark Companies, and the Town of Avon incorporated in 1978. A year later Avon dedicated 48 acres of open space in town and named it Harry A. Nottingham Park. The town built a dam to store water from Buck Creek as an emergency water supply—the birth of Nottingham Lake.

The paved path around Nottingham Lake offers a chance for a stroll, a picnic, and family time for everyone.

Miles and Directions

0.0 Start at the bulletin board in the northwest corner of the parking lot to the west of Town Hall (elevation: 7,440 feet). Go left first. (If you head right, read these directions in reverse.)

0.2 Come to a junction. Continue to the right around the lake.

0.3 Arrive at a T intersection. Turn right to continue around the lake.

0.45 Arrive at the junction to the fishing pier. The pier is about 265 feet down this spur trail. Return to the junction after enjoying the view from the pier.

0.7 Come to another junction. Turn right to continue around the lake. At the next intersection by the playground, turn right again.

0.8 Arrive back at the trailhead.

10 East Lake Creek Trail

The East Lake Creek Trail is a pleasant roller coaster through lush aspen forest with many types of bushes, including thimbleberry and elderberry. The hike travels about 1 mile to a set of switchbacks that drop down the side of the hill. This trail is beautiful in autumn when the aspen leaves turn gold and the many bushes show off their red berries and red, orange, and yellow leaves.

Distance: 2.0 miles out and back

Hiking time: 1 to 1.5 hours

Difficulty: Moderate due to a 480-foot elevation gain and constant undulations

Trail surface: Dirt

Best season: June through Oct

Other trail users: Equestrians

Canine compatibility: Dogs must be under voice control.

Fees and permits: None

Maps: USGS Grouse Mountain; Nat Geo Trails Illustrated 121 Eagle/Avon; Latitude 40° Vail and Eagle Trails; USFS White River National Forest map

Trail contact: USDA Forest Service, Eagle–Holy Cross Ranger District, 24747 US 24, Minturn 81645; (970) 827-5715; www.fs.usda.gov/whiteriver

Special considerations: Bring water with you because only small seeps and creeks are along the trail. Hunters may use this area during hunting season. The trail is neither marked nor maintained for winter use.

Finding the trailhead: From I-70 exit 163 (Edwards), head south into Edwards to US 6 and turn right. Drive for 0.7 mile and turn left by a church onto Lake Creek Road. In 1.9 miles turn right onto West Lake Creek Road, which is easy to miss. A brown sign says EAST LAKE TRAIL #1880 4 MILES. In another 1.6 miles the road turns to dirt. In another mile the road reaches a Y intersection—go left. In 1.2 miles turn left into the small parking lot just before the private property gate. No facilities are available at the trailhead. GPS: N39 35.14' / W106 35.74'

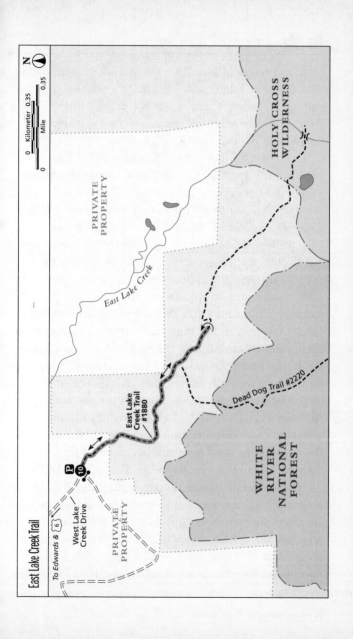

East Lake Creek Trail

The Hike

From the trailhead East Lake Creek Trail meanders about 12.5 miles up a long valley in the Sawatch Range before ending at Upper Camp Lake below 13,043-foot Eagle Peak. Along the way high alpine lakes feed small creeks that tumble into the main creek.

Orin Packard mined his claims along East Lake Creek back in 1893. By 1899 various property owners envisioned a metropolis in the area and called it Althea. Officially it was the Egley Mining District. The Packard Power and Mining Company worked its claims across the valley from the East Lake Milling and Mining Company (ELMMC), which several doctors and businessmen from Ohio owned. By 1905 the Packard Tunnel had been drilled in about 375 feet. By 1906 twenty men worked in the mines and the ELMMC had hand-drilled the Ohio Tunnel 650 feet into the mountain. The next year they installed a thirty-horsepower steam plant using a waterfall near the mines. Men used compressors to run their drills and also to power a sawmill to cut logs for the mine supports, flumes, and buildings. The goal was to drill the tunnel to reach lode claims such as the Washington. Although they reached the lode in around 1922 and found adequate gold, little ore was shipped from the area. The mines closed in the winter, and access was difficult. Today the ruins of many dreams lie silently along East Lake Creek.

You won't find mining remains during this hike, but the gold of the aspen is worth a fall hike! A group of aspen trees are really the same plant, sprouting new shoots from lateral roots. Therefore, some clumps of aspen are red, some gold, and some still green. Their decomposed leaves provide nutrients to the soil, enabling many other plants to grow into a lush garden.

Miles and Directions

0.0 Start at the East Lake Creek Trail bulletin board (elevation: 8,530 feet). The first 0.2 mile is through private property on an easement. Please stay on the trail.

0.2 Arrive at the PROPERTY BOUNDARY NATIONAL FOREST sign.

0.9 Come to the junction on the right with Dead Dog Trail #2220 (GPS: N39 34.75' / W106 35.23'). Continue straight ahead.

1.0 Arrive at a "wide" spot in the trail (GPS: N39 34.65' / W106 35.08'; elevation: 8,720 feet). From here the trail switchbacks and starts to descend steadily. This location is a good place to turn around and head back the way you came. (**Option:** You can continue as far as you like along the trail. The bridge over East Lake Creek at 3.2 miles, elevation 8,360 feet, is another good turnaround place for a more challenging hike—6.4 miles out and back with a 400-foot elevation gain on the way back, not counting all the undulations. The bridge is in the Holy Cross Wilderness. Dogs must be on leash. Please comply with wilderness regulations.)

2.0 Arrive back at the trailhead.

11 Julia's Deck

The trail to Julia's Deck is delightful and ADA accessible. Wonderful wildflowers line the gravel path, and it's easy to check out the various trees from wheelchair height or little legs. At the end of the trail is an accessible wooden deck with a roof-covered bench on one end and three benches in the middle. A gorgeous view of Mount of the Holy Cross rewards your journey.

Distance: 0.4 mile out and back
Hiking time: 15 to 30 minutes
Difficulty: Easy; ADA accessible with about a 20-foot elevation gain
Trail surface: Gravel and wood
Best season: Late June through Sept
Other trail users: None
Canine compatibility: Dogs must be under voice control.
Fees and permits: None
Maps: USGS Red Cliff; Nat Geo Trails Illustrated 108 Vail/Frisco/Dillon; Latitude 40° Vail and Eagle Trails; USFS White River National Forest map
Trail contact: USDA Forest Service, Eagle–Holy Cross Ranger District, 24747 US 24, Minturn 81645; (970) 827-5715; www.fs.usda.gov/whiteriver
Special considerations: No water is available along the trail. Shrine Pass Road is closed by snow in winter.

Finding the trailhead: From I-70 exit 190 (Shrine Pass Road/Red Cliff), head toward the rest area, but go straight onto the sometimes bumpy dirt road marked SHRINE PASS AND RED CLIFF (FR 709). Drive 3.8 miles to the Mount Holy Cross Overlook sign and turn left into the little parking area with an ADA-accessible vault toilet. GPS: N39 33.59' / W106 15.39'

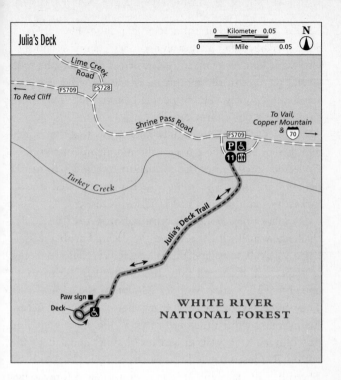

The Hike

In the 1800s various stories about a mountain with a "snowy cross" circulated around Colorado. The government-sponsored 1873 Hayden Survey set a goal to find this mysterious peak. By August the survey group, including photographer William Henry Jackson, arrived near present-day Minturn. The group ended up carrying Jackson's one hundred pounds of photographic gear on foot. Jackson used a wet glass plate camera. Not only was the "film" made of glass, which had to be handled carefully, but also Jackson needed to develop it soon after exposure. He carried a portable darkroom tent and all necessary chemicals and supplies with him. Arriving at a ridge across the valley, he took several pictures of the mountain, which caused a sensation across the country because people believed the snow-filled cross to be a sign from God.

A 1,500-foot vertical gully and a 750-foot horizontal rock bench create the cross on the mountain's eastern face. Collected snow causes the formation to stand out against the mountainside. The right arm has deteriorated due to rockslides, but a cross of snow still forms today.

In 1988 a new nonprofit organization, PAW (Physically-challenged Access to the Woods), partnered with the Vail-Eagle Valley Rotary and the White River National Forest to improve a little trail from the Shrine Pass Road to an opening with a good view of Mount of the Holy Cross. They built a viewing deck that wheelchairs could access. Aggie Young wrote the story of Paw, a kingly mountain lion that jumped a canyon, missed his landing, and fell to the bottom. He lost a toe and was paralyzed by his broken back. The other animals built an accessible path, and forest rangers gave him a wheelchair so he could return to his beloved woods. Julia Tuschman suggested creating Paw in costume, like Smokey Bear. Paw and Smokey visited many schools and appeared in parades. When Julia died, a wooden sign with the story of Paw and the deck were dedicated to her. PAW has evolved into Partners for Access to the Woods and continues to work on accessibility issues on public lands in partnership with various agencies.

Along the trail, take a moment to feel the needles of some trees. Spruce trees have sharp and square needles; you can roll the needles between your fingers. Fir tree needles are flat and friendly. The trail passes willows growing along a little creek and crosses a grassy meadow. Wildflowers create a colorful trail border. Some "pullouts," a stone bench, and the deck provide stopping places to enjoy your surroundings.

Miles and Directions

0.0 Start at the Mount of the HOLY CROSS OVERLOOK ¼ MILE sign with the wheelchair symbol (elevation: 10,680 feet).

0.15 Arrive at a stone bench. The trail curves left. Shortly the trail comes to a Y intersection; walk left for the ADA ramp. To the right is the sign with the story of Paw (notice the three toes on Paw's foot).

0.2 Arrive at Julia's Deck and enjoy the view (GPS: N39 33.48' / W106 15.53'). Return the way you came.

0.4 Arrive back at the trailhead.

12 Shrine Ridge Trail

Colorful, gorgeous, never-ending wildflowers and views make this trail a very popular hike. Mid-July to early August is typically the best time for the flower show. You may even enjoy a snowball fight at the drift just below Shrine Ridge. The views of the craggy Gore Range, Tenmile Range, and the Sawatch Range with the famous Mount of the Holy Cross are always spectacular. Remember the camera!

Distance: 4.1 miles out and back, with an option to extend the hike to 4.6 miles
Hiking time: 2 to 3.5 hours
Difficulty: More challenging due to a 771-foot elevation gain
Trail surface: Dirt
Best season: Early July through Sept
Other trail users: Equestrians
Canine compatibility: Dogs must be under voice control.
Fees and permits: None
Maps: USGS Vail Pass and Red Cliff; Nat Geo Trails Illustrated 108 Vail/Frisco/Dillon; Latitude 40° Vail and Eagle Trails; USFS White River National Forest map
Trail contact: USDA Forest Service, Eagle–Holy Cross Ranger

District, 24747 US 24, Minturn 81645; (970) 827-5715; www.fs.usda.gov/whiteriver
Special considerations: Water is not plentiful along this trail. Hunters use this area in the fall. In winter the Shrine Pass area is a favorite with both snowmobilers and backcountry skiers/snowboarders. The winter trailhead is near the Vail Pass Rest Area, and a daily fee is charged. A separate ski trail takes off from the first switchback on Shrine Pass Road.
Other: Please walk through any muddy spots and avoid trampling trailside vegetation. Staying on the trail also avoids spread of noxious weeds and prevents the trail from widening.

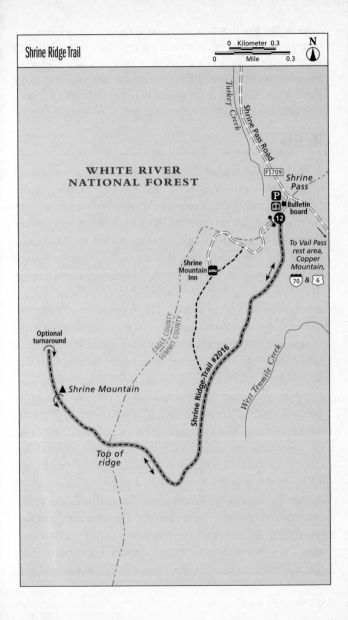

Finding the trailhead: From I-70 exit 190 (Vail Pass Rest Area), drive toward the rest area (restrooms if open, but water is not potable), but go straight ahead onto the sometimes bumpy dirt road marked SHRINE PASS AND RED CLIFF (FR 709). Drive approximately 2.3 miles to the top of Shrine Pass. Park in the parking lot on the south (left) side of the road. Vault toilets are available. GPS: N39 32.76' / W106 14.49'

The Hike

If you hike this trail at the peak of wildflower season, you're in for a real treat! Varieties of daisies, bistort, willows, Jacob's ladder, monkshood, chiming bells, and little red elephants bloom along the first part of the trail. After crossing a little creek, the trail starts to climb through forest with blackened stumps and tall stumps, probably the result of a large fire and logging activity in the late 1800s. Meadows painted in hues of yellow, red, and purple dazzle the eye. The little creek at about 1.0 mile is often bordered by magenta paintbrush, little red elephants, and Parry's primrose in shades of pink to purple.

Just below the final ascent to the ridge, a dense field of blue lupine blooms near the snowbanks. Watch for flying snowballs, as hikers enjoy snowball fights in midsummer.

Once you attain the ridge, wander along the trail to the right. As you walk, look to the left to see towering Mount of the Holy Cross. If snow lingers in the cracks, it's easy to see the cross that was once thought to be a sign from God. You can still see the cross if the snow has melted—you have to look a little harder. The wildflowers in the meadows are usually to die for. To the east the craggy Gore Range forms the border between Summit and Eagle Counties. The interesting red rock formations on the right are composed of the reddish conglomerate and sandstone of the Minturn Formation. About 300 million years ago, the Ancestral Rockies rose a little west of where today's Front Range lies. Colorado was situated near the equator in a tropical climate. As the mountains eroded, gray to red sediments came to rest in the shallow seas surrounding them. By the time the current Rockies rose, these sediments had metamorphosed into sandstone, shale, conglomerate, and marine limestone called the Minturn formation.

Shrine Mountain probably received its name from the fantastic view of Mount of the Holy Cross, once a national monument to which people made pilgrimages. The interesting red rock outcrops that remind people of shrines may be another source for its name.

Miles and Directions

0.0 Start at the bulletin board near the vault toilets in the parking lot (elevation: 11,089 feet). Walk southwest on the dirt road.

0.07 Turn left onto the singletrack trail at the Shrine Ridge Trail sign.

0.9 Arrive at the junction from the Shrine Mountain Inn coming in from the right. Continue straight ahead.

1.5 Look for a big flat rock along the right side of the trail as it climbs to the ridge. It offers a nice view of the Gore Range and is a good picture spot.

1.75 You may find a snowbank here just below the ridge. Enjoy! Climb a few more feet to the top of the ridge (GPS: N39 31.91' / W106 15.36'; elevation: 11,840 feet). Turn right to continue toward Shrine Mountain.

1.9 Pass a social trail coming in from the left. Continue straight ahead and enjoy the wildflowers and the view of Mount of the Holy Cross to the west.

2.05 Arrive at a trail sign (GPS: N39 32.06' / W106 15.55'). You can turn around here and return the way you came. (**Option:** Continue along the ridge for another 0.25 mile before turning around.)

4.1 Arrive back at the trailhead.

13 Wilder Gulch Trail

Search for the remains of Tom Wilder's cabin along this gentle subalpine trail. Travel along the creek, lined with willows, through open meadows with a few trees. Look for clues below to find the cabin remains in a wider spot in the valley.

Distance: 4.0 miles out and back

Hiking time: 2 to 3 hours

Difficulty: Moderate due to a 360-foot elevation gain

Trail surface: Dirt

Best season: Early July through Sept

Other trail users: Mountain bikers, equestrians

Canine compatibility: Dogs must be under voice control.

Fees and permits: None

Maps: USGS Vail Pass; Nat Geo Trails Illustrated 108 Vail/Frisco/Dillon; Latitude 40° Vail and Eagle Trails and Summit County Trails; USFS White River National Forest map

Trail contacts: USDA Forest Service, Dillon Ranger District, 680 Blue River Pkwy., Silverthorne 80498; (970) 468-5400; www.fs.usda.gov/whiteriver; www.dillonrangerdistrict.com

Special considerations: Bring your own water; the creek is not always near the trail, and creek water should be treated. Hunters may use this area during hunting season. In winter both snowmobilers and backcountry skiers/snowboarders enjoy this area. Wilder Gulch is groomed in winter for all users, and a daily fee is charged.

Other: Please walk through any muddy spots and avoid trampling trailside vegetation.

Finding the trailhead: From I-70 exit 190 (Vail Pass Rest Area), drive toward the rest area (restrooms if open, but water is not potable). Park in the upper parking lot. Walk down the stairs and head to the little building at the southeast end of the lower parking lot. Look for the obvious trail heading south to the right of the wastewater plant. GPS: N39 31.59' / W106 13.09'

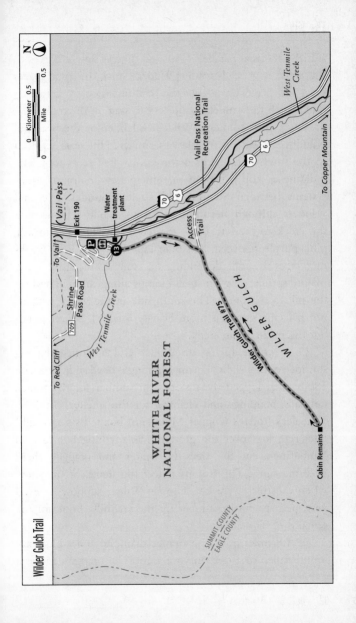

Wilder Gulch Trail

The Hike

Initially the trail parallels I-70, and then it slowly curves to the right as it heads toward Wilder Gulch. In some places grass and plants grow over the trail, but the way is easy to find. Watch for a mucky spot—try to stay on the trail.

Once you've entered Wilder Gulch, enjoy the beautiful wildflowers and open vistas. Ptarmigan Hill rears its head to the southwest, guarding the little valley at its foot. The building on top is part of the emergency communications systems between Summit and Eagle Counties. The trail wanders through beautiful meadows, while willows line the creek to the left. Look for red and yellow paintbrush, pink-purple fireweed, and blue lupine. A few little creeks may cross the trail, depending on available moisture. Trees, mainly spruce, grow in small clumps along the trail and on the hill to the north. The south side of the valley, with its north-facing slopes, is more heavily forested. Beaver ponds dot the meandering creek.

Once you're hiking up Wilder Gulch, notice the big stumps to the right. During mining's heyday in the late 1800s, men logged these slopes for lumber for the mines, railroads, buildings, and charcoal for the smelters. In 1885 Wheeler's (today's Copper Mountain) boasted six sawmills! Dragging logs over the ground was anything but easy, so lumbermen cut the trees in winter and dragged them over the snow. The stumps reflect the depth of the snow when the trees were cut. Thomas Wilder supposedly lived here, perhaps cutting timber for the sawmills. Look for the remains of his cabin!

At 1.8 miles notice an orange diamond and a blue diamond nailed to a tree on your right. The orange denotes a snowmobile route, while the blue signifies a cross-country skiing trail. You're getting close to the cabin remains.

In about 260 feet look for a large boulder on the right with a couple of trees that appear to grow out of it.

The trail passes by two clumps of trees. After the second clump the area along the trail widens a little more. Look to your left at the beaver ponds. Can you find the "flat" wooden planks near one of them?

Look to your right; at the edge of the trees, see if you can find the cabin ruins with a spruce tree growing out of them. Imagine living in such a small space!

Miles and Directions

0.0 Start at the edge of the pavement and the singletrack trail to the right of the wastewater plant (elevation: 10,560 feet).

0.04 Cross Tenmile Creek. The next section may have some wet areas, and the trail may be hard to spot. Continue heading south.

0.6 Arrive at the junction with the trail that starts at the Vail Pass National Recreation Trail (paved). Turn right and head up Wilder Gulch (GPS: N39 31.11' / W106 13.11').

2.0 Look to your right to find the cabin ruins with a spruce tree growing out of them (GPS: N39 30.47' / W106 14.30'; elevation: 10,920 feet). Turn around and return the way you came.

4.0 Arrive back at the trailhead.

14 Hallelujah Self-Guided Nature Trail

Enjoy an interpretive trail through spruce and fir forest along the edge of Copper Mountain's ski runs while learning about area history and life in the subalpine. To access the trailhead, ride up the American Eagle chairlift. Besides its being an easy way to reach the trail, you're rewarded with a bird's-eye view of the scenery around Copper Mountain.

Distance: 0.35-mile lollipop

Hiking time: 30 minutes to 1 hour

Difficulty: Moderate due to a 100-foot elevation gain in a short distance

Trail surface: Dirt and some rocks

Best season: Mid-June through Labor Day

Other trail users: None

Canine compatibility: Dogs are not allowed on the chairlift.

Fees and permits: Chairlift ticket required

Schedule: The American Eagle lift operates from 10 a.m. to 4 p.m. mid-June through Labor Day, weather permitting.

Maps: USGS Copper Mountain; Nat Geo Trails Illustrated 109 Breckenridge/Tennessee Pass;

Latitude 40° Summit County Trails; USFS White River National Forest map

Trail contacts: Copper Mountain Resort, 209 Ten Mile Circle, Copper Mountain 80443; (866) 841-2481; www.coppercolorado.com

USDA Forest Service, Dillon Ranger District, 680 Blue River Pkwy., Silverthorne 80498; (970) 468-5400; www.fs.usda.gov/whiteriver; www.dillonrangerdistrict.com

Special considerations: Bring water, as none is available along the trail. Restrooms, water, and food are available in Solitude Station near the top of the American Eagle lift.

Finding the trailhead: From I-70 exit 195 (Copper Mountain/Leadville), head south and turn right at the traffic light. In 0.6 mile turn left onto Ten Mile Circle. In 0.1 mile turn left and then right into covered parking. Or

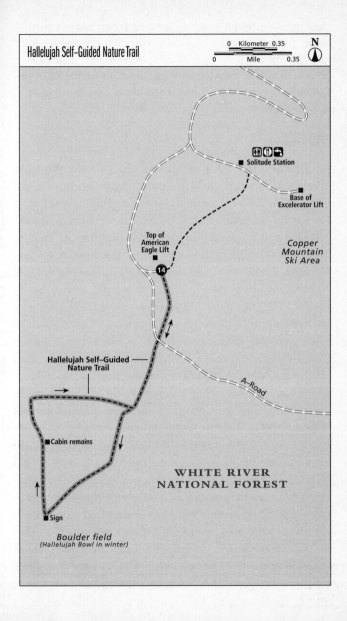

Hallelujah Self-Guided Nature Trail

0   Kilometer 0.35

0   Mile   0.35

N

🚻🍴🧺 ■ Solitude Station

■ Base of
Excelerator Lift

Copper
Mountain
Ski Area

Top of
American
Eagle Lift
■
14

Hallelujah Self-Guided ──
Nature Trail

A-Road

■ Cabin remains

WHITE RIVER
NATIONAL FOREST

■ Sign

Boulder field
(Hallelujah Bowl in winter)

you can drive another 0.1 mile around the traffic circle and park in the upper parking deck. Walk into the Center Village and look straight ahead for a sign directing you to Guest Services, where you need to obtain a chairlift pass. Water and restrooms are located in this building. When you get off the American Eagle lift, walk straight ahead and a tad left to the path lined with wood. GPS: N39 28.98' / W106 09.39'

The Hike

Copper Mountain has seen many changes over the years. Prehistoric Indians and Utes passed by, traveling over Vail Pass in search of the plentiful game that grazed where Dillon Reservoir sits today. After miners found gold near Breckenridge in 1859, hopeful prospectors spread across Summit County. A few men successfully mined the slopes of Copper Mountain. One energetic miner dug a shaft at the summit, finding low-grade copper ore, hence the mountain's name.

In 1879 Judge John S. Wheeler purchased 320 acres, now part of Copper Mountain Resort, and started a hay ranch. The next year silver miners arrived, and the ranch became a town known by various names: Wheeler's Ranch, Wheeler Station, Wheeler's, Wheeler, and Wheeler Junction. Wheeler Junction prospered, with a hotel, saloons, a post office, and several sawmills. In 1884 the Colorado & Southern Railroad finished laying tracks to Wheeler Junction on the east side of Tenmile Creek. Its railroad station at Wheeler was named Solitude Station. On the other side of the creek, the Denver & Rio Grande railroad built its line with a station called Wheeler's.

The mining era passed, and the town began to return to the earth. Sheepherders tended their flocks on grassy slopes near the abandoned town from 1905 to 1979.

By 1960 investors started to contact the USDA Forest Service about developing a ski area at Copper Mountain.

Inquiries came without any follow-up. Finally, in 1968, a group of investors formed Copper Mountain Associates and purchased 280 acres at the mountain's base (part of the Wheeler Ranch). Chuck Lewis, a former executive vice president of Vail Associates, became the general partner. The group obtained a ski area permit from the forest service, arranged financing, and started construction in 1971. In December 1972 dedication ceremonies signaled the opening of "the most nearly perfect ski mountain in the United States."

As you hike up the Hallelujah Nature Trail, not long after the SURVIVAL IN THE SUBALPINE sign, look to your left at the boulder field. Deep snows in winter transform the boulder field into Hallelujah Bowl, an expert ski run. Imagine what life is like for the tiny pika, which lives in the boulder field year-round, munching on its supply of flowers and grass throughout the winter. With some luck you may see the little rabbit-family members gathering their food cache.

Miles and Directions

0.0 Start at the beginning of the Hallelujah Self-Guided Nature Trail (elevation: 11,250 feet).

0.05 Cross the road and walk straight ahead to continue on the trail.

0.1 Arrive at a junction. Walk to your left to the SURVIVAL IN THE SUBALPINE sign.

0.15 Turn right at the EDGE OF THE ALPINE sign (GPS: N39 28.87' / W106 09.45'; elevation: 11,350 feet). At the next junction go right (look for the arrow in the tree).

0.2 Arrive at cabin remains. Continue on the trail to the left of the cabin.

0.25 Turn left at the end of the loop and return the way you came.

0.35 Arrive back at the trailhead.

15 Masontown

The hike starts on the paved recreation path that follows the route of the defunct Colorado & Southern Railroad and passes by the old Frisco Tunnel. The Mount Royal Trail to Masontown is rather steep, so take your time. The hike is worth the effort! Explore the interesting remains of the former mining town and mill, which nature is slowly reclaiming.

Distance: 2.0 miles out and back
Hiking time: 1 to 1.5 hours
Difficulty: More challenging due to a 490-foot elevation gain
Trail surface: Paved recreational path and dirt trail
Best season: June through Oct
Other trail users: Mountain bikers, equestrians on dirt trail; bicyclists, walkers, longboarders, joggers on paved recreational path
Canine compatibility: Dogs must be leashed on paved recreational path; under voice control on dirt trail.
Fees and permits: None
Maps: USGS Frisco; Nat Geo Trails Illustrated 108 Vail/Frisco/

Dillon; Latitude 40° Summit County Trails; USFS White River National Forest map
Trail contact: USDA Forest Service, Dillon Ranger District, 680 Blue River Pkwy., Silverthorne 80498; (970) 468-5400; www.fs .usda.gov/whiteriver; www.dillon rangerdistrict.com
Special considerations: Bring your own water—none is available along the trail. Hunters may use this area during hunting season. Be aware of avalanche danger near and above Masontown in winter. These trails are neither marked nor maintained for winter use.

Finding the trailhead: From I-70 exit 201 (Frisco Main Street), drive east approximately 0.1 mile toward town to a parking lot on your right (south). Turn right into the parking lot. Portable toilets are usually available at the trailhead in the summer. Summit Stage bus stops are located close to the trailhead. GPS: N39 34.49' / W106 06.66'

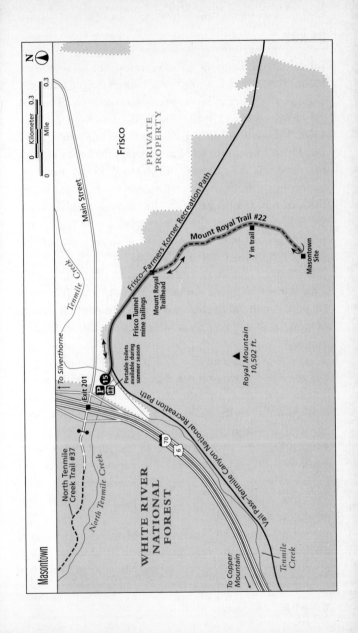

Masontown

N

To Silverthorne

Exit 201

Main Street

Tenmile Creek

15

P

Portable toilets available during summer season

Frisco Tunnel mine tailings

Frisco–Farmers Korner Recreation Path

Mount Royal Trailhead

Mount Royal Trail #22

Frisco

PRIVATE PROPERTY

Y in trail

Masontown Site

North Tenmile Creek Trail #37

North Tenmile Creek

70

6

Vail Pass–Tenmile Canyon National Recreation Path

WHITE RIVER NATIONAL FOREST

To Copper Mountain

Tenmile Creek

Royal Mountain 10,502 ft.

0   Kilometer   0.3
0   Mile   0.3

The Hike

While walking along the paved recreational path toward the Mount Royal Trail, imagine the sounds of the old trains that steamed along here. Two railroads served Frisco. The first, the Denver & Rio Grande (D&RG), came from Leadville down Tenmile Canyon, arriving in town in summer 1882. The Denver, South Park & Pacific, later called the Colorado & Southern (C&S), chooed and chugged down today's recreational path from Breckenridge, arriving in Frisco in July 1883. At mile 0.3 the depot for the C&S once stood. Across the field you can see the tailings from the Frisco Tunnel, which operated into the 1930s. The D&RG ended service in 1911, while the C&S ran until 1937.

In 1866 General Buford discovered gold and copper leads above Rainbow Lake on the side of Royal Mountain. He built a mill, and the little town called Masontown started to grow. In 1880 the Victoria Mine produced about $10,000 in gold.

The *Summit County Journal*'s June 4, 1904, issue reported that the Masontown mill was fully operational with electric lighting and "runs with the accuracy of a watch." A tram brought ore from the mine to the mill. A complex process produced gold amalgam, cyanide precipitates, and auriferous sulfides. The first two became gold bars, and the concentrates were shipped to smelters. The paper further reported the ore's value at $5 to $20 per ton in gold, while the costs of mining and milling ran about $3 per ton. Frisco mining played out about 1910.

Some legends say that while Masontown's residents partied in Frisco on New Year's Eve in 1912, a snow slide roared down Mount Victoria, taking Masontown's buildings with it. Other accounts relate that the snow slide that wiped out Masontown occurred in 1926, leaving only a few cabins on the north side. You can still see the scar of the avalanche today.

Make sure to take some time to explore the area of Masontown. Old metal bands, a brick floor, and other interesting items can be found. Please leave relics for others to enjoy.

Miles and Directions

0.0 Start at the bulletin board before the bridge (elevation: 9,110 feet). Walk across the bridge. At the junction with the paved recreation path, turn left.

0.25 Look to your right across an open area. The big mine tailings are the remains of the Frisco Tunnel.

0.4 Arrive at the start of the Mount Royal Trail on the right (GPS: N39 34.35' / W106 06.27'). Read the signs and bulletin board for more information about the area. The trail climbs fairly steeply from here. Ignore any trails coming in from the left as you hike.

0.8 Come to a junction. Continue uphill to the right.

0.9 Arrive at a hunk of metal and some mining holes in the ground. The trail appears to go in three directions; take the middle path. The trail is lined with small rocks.

1.0 A trail goes to the left. Continue uphill a little more to the flat top of a tailings pile. Enjoy the view of Grays Peak, Torreys Peak, part of Frisco, and a little of Dillon Reservoir (GPS: N39 33.91' / W106 06.23'; elevation: 9,600 feet). Return the way you came.

2.0 Arrive back at the trailhead.

16 X10U8 and B&B Loop

Take a stroll past historic mines and the remains of an old gold dredge. Interpretive signs explain the sites. The sides of French Gulch sport golden wounds of mine tailings, while the bottom is filled with boulder piles dredged from the creek bottom in the endless quest for gold.

Distance: 2.4-mile loop, including several short spurs
Hiking time: 1 to 2 hours
Difficulty: Moderate due to a 240-foot elevation gain
Trail surface: Dirt trails and old wagon roads
Best season: June through Oct
Other trail users: Mountain bikers, equestrians
Canine compatibility: Dogs must be on leash.
Fees and permits: None
Maps: USGS Breckenridge; Nat Geo Trails Illustrated 109 Breckenridge/Tennessee Pass; Latitude 40° Summit County Trails; Breckenridge & Summit County Hiking and Biking Trail Map
Trail contact: Town of Breckenridge Open Space and Trails, 150 Ski Hill Rd., Breckenridge 80424; (970) 453-3160; www.townof breckenridge.com
Special considerations: Bring water with you, as none is available along the trail.
Other: You can snowshoe or cross-country ski this loop in the winter. Both trailhead parking lots are plowed in winter.

Finding the trailhead: From I-70 exit 203 (Frisco/Breckenridge), head south on CO 9 for 9.5 miles. Turn left onto CR 450 at the 7-Eleven store. In 0.3 mile turn right onto Reiling Road. In another 0.7 mile turn left onto French Gulch Road. Drive 1.1 miles to the B&B Mines Trailhead. Turn right into the parking lot. No facilities are available. GPS: N39 29.04' / W106 00.59'

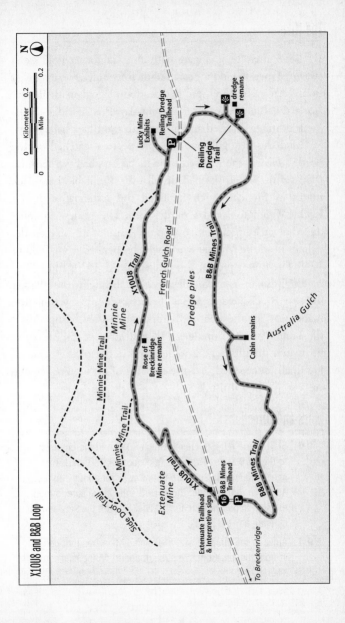

X10U8 and B&B Loop

N

Kilometer
0   0.2

Mile
0   0.2

To Breckenridge

16 B&B Mines Trailhead
P
Extenuate Trailhead & Interpretive sign
X10U8 Trail
B&B Mines Trail
Extenuate Mine
Side Door Trail
Minnie Mine Trail
Minnie Mine
Minnie Mine Trail
X10U8 Trail
Rose of Breckenridge Mine remains
French Gulch Road
Dredge piles
Cabin remains
Australia Gulch
B&B Mines Trail
B&B Mines Trail
Lucky Mine Exhibits
Reiling Dredge Trailhead
P
Reiling Dredge Trail
dredge remains

The Hike

By 1858 men discouraged with the California gold fields swarmed to Colorado in search of their fortunes. Heading west from Denver in 1859, prospectors found gold in their pans along the Blue River near present-day Breckenridge. Hundreds of miners arrived and spread into the Blue's tributaries.

After the easy gold ran out, prospectors searched on the nearby hills for the source of the metal that had washed into the streams. Mines popped up all over. Profitable hard-rock mines in French Gulch included the Extenuate, Minnie, Lucky, Wellington, and Country Boy. The mines also produced silver, lead, and zinc over time. At mile 0.6 you cross the tailings from the Minnie Mine, which operated from 1880 to 1958. The mine's production peaked in the 1920s and 1930s.

Englishman Ben Stanley Revett brought the dredge boat to Breckenridge. A San Francisco company built the machinery for the floating barges, while Revett supervised the building of the dredges. His first attempts failed, being no match for the large boulders and depth of the deposits. He finally succeeded, and the remains of his Reiling dredge are a stop along this hike.

Miles and Directions

0.0 Start at the edge of French Gulch Road and the entrance to the B&B Mines Trailhead (elevation: 9,960 feet). Turn right onto French Gulch Road and walk for about 225 feet, and then turn left onto the X10U8 Trail. Make sure to read the sign about the Extenuate Mine. Stay on the singletrack, ignoring any old roads.

0.4 Arrive at the junction with the Minnie Mine Trail that comes in from the left. Continue straight ahead on the singletrack X10U8 Trail.

0.5 Come to the Rose of Breckenridge Mine remains and interpretive sign.

0.6 Cross the bottom of the Minnie Mine tailings.

0.8 Arrive at the junction of the X10U8 and Minnie Mine Trails. Turn right onto the Minnie Mine Trail (old wagon road).

0.9 Turn left and hike up the Interpretive Trail. Partway up on the left is a sign about the Lucky Mine. At the top is an exhibit of equipment from the Lucky Mine concentration mill jig (elevation: 10,200 feet). Return the way you came, and turn left at the old wagon road.

1.0 Pass through the fence at the Minnie Mine Trail trailhead. Walk across the Reiling Dredge Trailhead parking lot, cross French Gulch Road, and you'll see the sign for the Reiling Dredge Trail (GPS: N39 29.11' / W105 59.78').

1.2 Turn left at the split-rail fence. Walk about 100 feet to the interpretive sign and view the remains of the Reiling dredge. Return the way you came and turn left onto the main trail.

1.3 Turn left to go to the viewing platform for another view of the dredge remains, return to the main trail, and turn left. Walk about 250 feet and come to the three-way junction of Reiling Dredge, Turk's, and B&B Mines Trails. Go straight ahead on the doubletrack B&B Mines Trail.

1.8 Turn left at an unmarked junction to see the remains of an old cabin. Return to the main trail and turn left.

2.0 Come to the junction of Turk's and B&B Mines Trails. Continue straight ahead. At the next junction stay to the right.

2.1 Arrive at the junction with the V3 Trail. Head downhill to the right.

2.2 Come to the junction with B&B Spur Trail. Continue straight ahead.

2.4 Arrive back at the B&B Mines Trailhead parking lot.

17 Iowa Hill Trail

Explore the historic Iowa Hill Hydraulic Placer Mine along this interpretive trail with interesting exhibits. The hikes takes you back more than a century to the days when miners panned for gold and then developed techniques using water cannons, called hydraulic giants, to wash the sides of gulches into sluice boxes to capture gold particles. *Mining History News* rates this trail as "one of the best hydraulic mining exhibits in the world."

Distance: 1.0-mile lollipop, including several spurs
Hiking time: 1 to 1.5 hours
Difficulty: Moderate due to a 190-foot elevation gain in a short distance
Trail surface: Dirt
Best season: Late May through late Oct (snowshoe in winter)
Other trail users: None
Canine compatibility: Dogs must be on leash.
Fees and permits: None
Maps: USGS Frisco; Nat Geo Trails Illustrated 108 Vail/Frisco/Dillon; Latitude 40° Summit County Trails; Breckenridge & Summit County Hiking and Biking Trail Map
Trail contact: Town of Breckenridge, 150 Ski Hill Rd.,
Breckenridge 80424; (970) 453-3160; www.townofbreckenridge.com
Special considerations: No water is available along the trail. If the trail is muddy, please walk through the mud puddles and not on the vegetation around the trail. Trampled vegetation results in bigger mud puddles! The trail is neither marked nor maintained for winter use, and the trailhead is not plowed. Please stay on the trail to avoid trespassing on nearby private properties.
Other: The Breckenridge Heritage Alliance offers tours of the boardinghouse year-round (www.breckheritage.com or 970-453-9767, ext. 7).

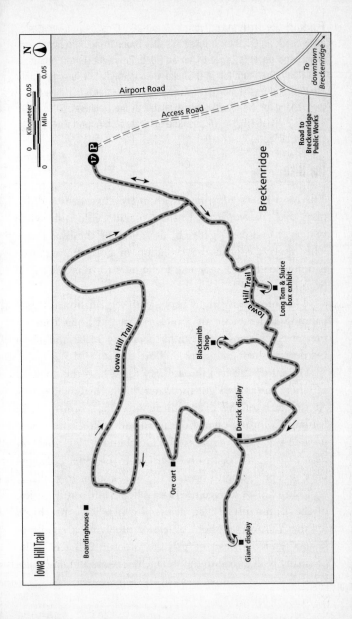

Iowa Hill Trail

Finding the trailhead: From I-70 exit 203 (Frisco/Breckenridge), drive south on CO 9 for 9 miles to Valley Brook Road. Turn right (west) and travel 0.2 mile to Airport Road. Turn right (north) on Airport Road, then turn left in 0.3 mile, then immediately turn right onto the dirt road by the Iowa Hill Trailhead sign. Drive north 0.1 mile to the parking lot. No facilities are available at the trailhead. GPS: N39 30.14' / W106 03.14'. (A bus stop is located on Airport Road. close to the trailhead.)

The Hike

The Iowa Hill Trail is lined with interpretive signs and displays that take you back to the Colorado gold rush, when miners chased their "get rich" dreams along the Blue River. The displays explain the evolution of gold mining from panning streams to hydraulic techniques for removing gold from the hills.

The interpretive signs begin with explanations of gold panning and the use of a rocker box and Long Tom for greater efficiency. Other exhibits include a blacksmith shop, old derrick, hydraulic giant, and ore car.

Hiking up the trail through dry forest begs the question of where the miners got the water for the hydraulic giants. At the turn of the twentieth century, the Banner Placer Mining Company owned the mine and built a reservoir to provide water. According to the October 15, 1904, *Breckenridge Bulletin,* the company, managed by Colonel L. Kingsbury, was preparing to operate the well-known Iowa placer on Iowa Hill. "A storage reservoir is being built on a portion of the Boom placer (ten acres of which were purchased for that purpose) to hold water for supplying a couple of 'giants' under a head of pressure of over 200 feet." The company built a road to the storage reservoirs and dug miles of ditches to make the hydraulic placer operation a success. The water dropped over 200 feet in elevation through a 3,200-foot-long, 22-inch steel pipe to the Iowa placers. The pressure generated was estimated at 260 pounds per square inch. Lateral pipes ran three 6-inch nozzles, which played on the 18- to 40-foot-high gravel banks. The gravel passed through a 4-foot-wide sluice with riffles that caught the gold. A dynamo run by water generated power for lights for night work.

At the top of loop is the Miners' Boarding House, dating back to at least 1876. Hike back in time and learn about some of Breckenridge's mining history.

Miles and Directions

0.0 Start at the Iowa Hill Trail bulletin board (elevation: 9,450 feet).

0.06 The trail comes to a Y intersection. Turn left (south) and follow the trail that leads you to many interpretive signs. Take time to explore the side trails to several signs and displays.

0.4 The trail reaches a Y. Turn left (west) to the hydraulic giant display and sign and then return to the junction and the derrick interpretive sign. Head uphill from here.

0.6 The trail reaches another Y. Turn right and head down to the Miners' Boarding House. Continue on the downhill trail (GPS: N39 30.13' / W106 03.30'; elevation: 9,640 feet).

1.0 Arrive back at the trailhead.

18 Osprey Viewpoint

Enjoy an easy, ADA-accessible walk to a little peninsula with a spotting scope for observing the osprey nest on Sentinel Island. The east end of the island is closed during nesting season to minimize disturbing the birds. Ospreys live around open water, where they dive-bomb fish seen from high above, grabbing their dinner with outstretched talons.

Distance: 0.9 mile out and back, with one spur
Hiking time: 30 minutes to 1 hour
Difficulty: Easy; ADA accessible with about a 30-foot elevation change
Trail surface: Paved recreation path with a little gravel at overlook
Best season: Early May through Oct
Other trail users: Bicyclists, joggers
Canine compatibility: Dogs must be on leash.
Fees and permits: None
Maps: USGS Frisco; Nat Geo Trails Illustrated 108 Vail/Frisco/Dillon; Latitude 40° Summit County Trails; USFS White River National Forest map; Breckenridge & Summit County Hiking and Biking Trail Map
Trail contacts: USDA Forest Service, Dillon Ranger District, 680 Blue River Pkwy., Silverthorne 80498; (970) 468-5400; www.fs.usda.gov/whiteriver; www.dillonrangerdistrict.com
Summit County Open Space and Trails, County Commons, 0037 Peak One Dr., SCR 1005, Frisco 80443; (970) 668-4060; www.co.summit.co.us
Special considerations: Bring your own water. The rec path is snow-covered in winter: Ski, snowshoe, or walk.

Finding the trailhead: From I-70 exit 203 (Frisco/Breckenridge), drive south to the first traffic light and turn left on Dillon Dam Road. Drive 1.8 miles and look for a large dirt parking area on the right

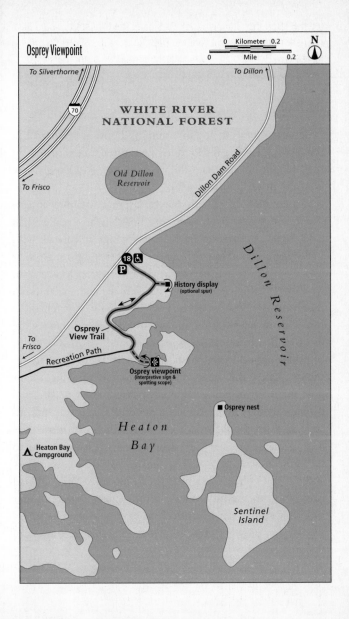

(past Heaton Bay Campground). Park here. The hike starts where the rec path turns east away from the Dam Road at the SUMMIT COUNTY RECREATIONAL PATHWAY sign. No facilities are available at the trailhead. GPS: N39 36.50' / W106 04.29'

The Hike

A definite sign of spring in Summit County is the return of the ospreys. Fishing for food in open water, they return from their winter homes when the ice on Dillon Reservoir melts, typically in early to mid-May.

Sometimes called fish hawks, ospreys mainly eat fish. Their wings span 5 or more feet, but they are smaller than bald eagles. Both sexes have brown wings and backs with white bellies, a curved beak, and a black stripe through their eyes. When soaring, they bend their wings, so look for an M-shape floating in the sky. Excellent eyesight enables an osprey to spot fish under the water. Diving, it catches the fish with its talons. After the catch the osprey arranges the fish headfirst to minimize wind resistance.

Ospreys build their nests in open areas for easy access. Unfortunately, the skinny and often densely growing lodge-pole pines surrounding Dillon Reservoir don't make good nesting stands. The platform on Sentinel Island was built to provide a sturdy platform for a nest, which can grow to 6 feet in diameter over time. Osprey pairs usually return to the same nest each year. The female lays up to four eggs, and the chicks hatch in a little over a month. Mom and Dad bring food to the little ones until they fledge after another month. Ospreys can live fifteen to twenty years. The interpretive sign provides more information about the ospreys of Sentinel Island.

Dillon Reservoir is a man-made lake, providing water for thirsty residents on the dry eastern plains in the Denver Metro area. Three rivers fill the reservoir: the Snake River, the Blue River, and Tenmile Creek. Dam construction started in April 1960. The earthen dam required twelve million tons of fill dirt. Workers completed the dam in July 1963, and water storage began in September of that year. Dillon Reservoir has a 24.5-mile shoreline and can store about 85.5 billion gallons of water.

Enjoy your walk and the views of the Tenmile Range. Hopefully you'll see an osprey or two!

Miles and Directions

0.0 Start where the rec path turns east off the Dillon Dam Road (elevation: 9,050 feet).

0.1 Arrive at the junction with a spur trail on the left to an interpretive sign about area history (optional 425-foot spur).

0.4 Turn left at the spur trail to the osprey viewpoint.

0.45 Arrive at the spotting scope and the interpretive sign about ospreys (GPS: N39 36.29' / W106 04.22'). Return the way you came.

0.9 Arrive back at the trailhead.

19 Dillon Peninsula

This mostly flat, gated dirt road to the west portal of the Roberts Tunnel is hikable year-round. Because this trail is lower in elevation than many trails in central Summit County, the snow melts faster and the flowers bloom earlier here. Keep your eyes open for foxes, pine squirrels, deer, red-tailed hawks, and ospreys. Enjoy the beautiful views of the Gore Range and the Tenmile Range across the blue waters of Dillon Reservoir. Snowshoe, walk, or ski in the winter.

Distance: 2.9 miles out and back

Hiking time: 1 to 1.5 hours

Difficulty: Easy due to a 130-foot elevation change

Trail surface: Dirt road and paved recreation path

Best season: Year-round

Other trail users: None

Canine compatibility: Dogs must be on leash.

Fees and permits: None

Maps: USGS Frisco; Nat Geo Trails Illustrated 108 Vail/Frisco/Dillon; Latitude 40° Summit County Trails; USFS White River National Forest map

Trail contact: Town of Dillon, 275 Lake Dillon Dr., Dillon 80435; (970) 468-2403; www.townofdillon.com

Special considerations: Bring water, as only Dillon Reservoir contains water along the trail.

Other: This trail is the access road for Denver Water, so you may occasionally see a vehicle on it.

Finding the trailhead: From I-70 exit 205 (Silverthorne/Dillon), head east on US 6 toward Dillon. Drive 3.6 miles to just past mile marker 212. Turn right and drive 0.1 mile into the parking lot. The turnoff is across US 6 from Cemetery Road. No facilities are available at the trailhead. GPS: N39 36.65' / W106 01.34'

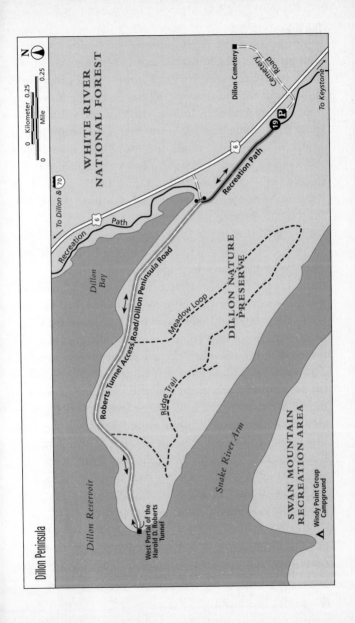

Dillon Peninsula

The Hike

This peninsula, which juts out into Dillon Reservoir along the Snake River inlet, has seen many changes over time. Bison, deer, elk, and antelope once grazed in the lush valley, now covered by water. Indians, mainly Utes, followed the game here in summer. Mountain men once rendezvoused in La Bonte's Hole, where the Snake and Blue Rivers and Tenmile Creek converged. (Today the confluence lies underwater southeast of Dillon Dam.) La Bonte the man remains a mystery—perhaps a French-Canadian trapper lent his name to the area.

The gold rush in the 1860s brought miners to the south and east of La Bonte's Hole. By the early 1870s entrepreneurs had built a stage stop and trading post near the confluence of the three rivers. Homesteaders around Dillon and down the Lower Blue Valley grew crops and raised cattle to sell to the miners and other Summit County residents. The Denver & Rio Grande railroad reached Dillon in 1882, and the rival Denver, South Park, and Pacific arrived in 1883. The town of Dillon incorporated on January 26, 1883, on the northeast side of the Snake River. But Dillon soon moved just south of the confluence of the three rivers to be closer to both railroads. Citizens moved their town (the third time) west of Tenmile Creek but still close to transportation. Dillon became a hub for the ranches and farms of the area. Herds of cattle bound for Denver were driven along roads to the Dillon depot. Ore and lumber hauled by wagon to the town were loaded onto trains for transport.

As early as 1910 the Denver Water Board (DWB) drew plans to divert water from the Blue River drainage to the eastern slope for growing Denver and started buying water rights on the western slope. In 1927 plans were filed showing a dam across the Blue River just below the three-river confluence. A 23.3-mile tunnel would transport the water to the South Platte River and on to Denver. When times were tough during the depression, DWB purchased many properties in and around Dillon at tax sales. Dam construction started in April 1960. The earthen dam required twelve million tons of fill dirt. Dillon moved a fourth time to a hill to the north. More than 300 graves had to be moved from the Dillon Cemetery, established in 1885, to the new cemetery along US 6.

The Harold D. Roberts Tunnel is named for an attorney and special counsel for DWB. Workers finished the dam in July 1963, and water storage began in September. Dillon Reservoir has a 24.5-mile shoreline and can store about 85.5 billion gallons of water.

Miles and Directions

0.0   Start at the gate at the north end of the parking lot (elevation: 9,070 feet). Turn right (northwest) on the paved rec path.

0.3   Come to a dirt road and bulletin board. Turn left past the bulletin board onto the dirt road and past the gate (GPS: N39 36.84' / W106 01.60').

1.45   Arrive at the end of the road near the west portal of the Roberts Tunnel (GPS: N39 37.03' / W106 02.69'; elevation: 9,040 feet). Return the way you came.

2.9   Arrive back at the parking lot.

20 Lily Pad Lake Trail

This gentle climb to pretty Lily Pad Lake is a treat for the whole family. The trail passes through typically dry lodgepole pine forest with sparse vegetation. Several ponds, a creek, and other wet areas produce tall grasses, willows, and wildflowers. A smaller lake is almost covered in pond lilies, while the larger lake supports a few of the plants along with an old beaver lodge.

Distance: 3.3 miles out and back
Hiking time: 1.5 to 2.5 hours
Difficulty: Moderate due to a 176-foot elevation gain
Trail surface: Dirt
Best season: June through Oct
Other trail users: Equestrians
Canine compatibility: Dogs must be on leash.
Fees and permits: None. Limit of fifteen people per group.
Schedule: Year-round. Ski, snowshoe, or walk the trail in winter.
Maps: USGS Frisco; Nat Geo Trails Illustrated 108 Vail/Frisco/Dillon; Latitude 40° Summit County Trails; USFS White River National Forest map

Trail contact: USDA Forest Service, Dillon Ranger District, 680 Blue River Pkwy., Silverthorne 80498; (970) 468-5400; www.fs.usda.gov/whiteriver; www.dillonrangerdistrict.com
Special considerations: Bring water, as none is readily available for most of the hike. Hunters may use this area during hunting season. The trail is neither marked nor maintained for winter use but is usually easy to follow due to frequent use.
Other: The trail is mainly within the Eagles Nest Wilderness area. Please comply with wilderness regulations.

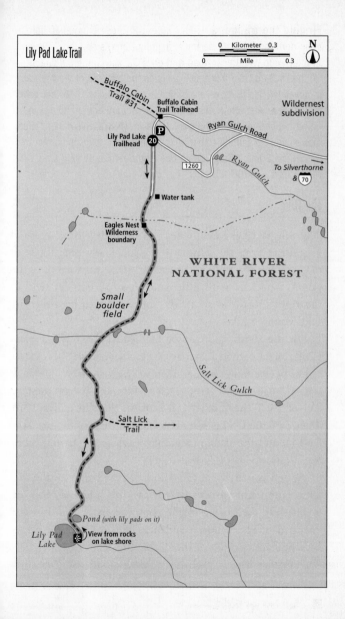

Lily Pad Lake Trail

0   Kilometer   0.3

0   Mile   0.3

N

Buffalo Cabin Trail #31

Buffalo Cabin Trail Trailhead

Wildernest subdivision

Lily Pad Lake Trailhead

P
20

Ryan Gulch Road

1260

Ryan Gulch

To Silverthorne & 70

■ Water tank

Eagles Nest Wilderness boundary ■

WHITE RIVER NATIONAL FOREST

Small boulder field

Salt Lick Gulch

Salt Lick Trail

Pond (with lily pads on it)

Lily Pad Lake

View from rocks on lake shore

Finding the trailhead: From I-70 exit 205 (Silverthorne/Dillon), head north on CO 9 to the traffic light by Wendy's and the 7-Eleven. Turn left onto Wildernest Road and drive 3.5 miles. The parking lot for the Lily Pad Lake Trail trailhead is on the left side of the road as it curves left. No facilities are available at the trailhead. To reach the trailhead, walk south on the road to where another road comes in from the right. You'll see the trailhead sign. (**Note**: This parking area also serves the Buffalo Cabin Trail, so be sure to find the correct trailhead.) The Summit Stage has a bus stop near the parking area. GPS: N39 37.14' / W106 06.63'

The Hike

The Lily Pad Lake Trail takes you through various types of vegetation from the almost-sterile lodgepole pine forest to tall wildflowers growing in wetter areas. Explore the little ponds, especially with little ones. A small boulder field to the right (north) at about 0.6 mile seems to be a favorite with younger hikers.

To the south and east of Lily Pad Lake, the Giberson family once owned 720 acres where they raised beef cattle, ten to twelve milk cows, and ten to twelve horses. The ranch started small at 160 acres in 1909. Through the Homestead Act of 1862, they added 160 acres to their spread in 1916. They paid the US government to graze their cattle on all the land behind the ranch, including the lake the family called Pond Lily (today's Lily Pad Lake).

When you arrive at Lily Pad Lake, the bigger of the two lakes, you might wonder why it has only a few lily pads on it. The lake used to be smaller, but beavers built a dam and enlarged it. The yellow pond lilies did not like the bigger lake, perhaps because of the change in depth or water flow. The smaller lake is probably a kettle pond left over from glacial times and sports a large quantity of yellow pond lilies. Mother ducks and little ducklings like the little lake, and the ducklings walk over the lily pads. Pine beetles killed the lodgepole pine trees around the lakes, but spruce, fir, and little pines still add some green to the scene.

Miles and Directions

0.0 Start at the Lily Pad Lake Trail bulletin board (elevation: 9,800 feet). The walk up the dirt road to the water tank may seem steep, but the trail is gentler once it becomes a singletrack.

0.3 Enter the Eagles Nest Wilderness.

0.6 Arrive at a small boulder field to the right, a good place for kids to scramble.

1.1 Come to the junction with Salt Lick Trail. Continue straight on Lily Pad Lake Trail (GPS: N39 36.33' / W106 06.82').

1.6 Arrive at Lily Pad Lake. The pond to your left has pond lilies. The lake straight ahead is Lily Pad Lake. Stop here, or continue on the trail between the lakes for a view north.

1.65 Come to some nice rocks on the right with a view of the lake and Buffalo Mountain (GPS: N39 35.97' / W106 06.93'; elevation: 9,880 feet). Look for the old beaver lodge near the southwest shore. Return the way you came.

3.3 Arrive back at the trailhead.

Area Clubs and Trail Groups

Clubs

Colorado Mountain Club Gore Range Group

www.cmc.org/groups/groups_gorerange.aspx

Colorado's main hiking/climbing club is the Colorado Mountain Club. The state offices are located in Golden. The Gore Range Group serves members in Eagle and Summit Counties.

Trail Groups (Education, Trail Maintenance, Advocacy)

Colorado Trail Foundation

710 10th St. #210, Golden 80401; (303) 384-3729; www.coloradotrail.org

CTF works in partnership with the USDA Forest Service and other agencies to maintain the Colorado Trail with volunteer work crews and educational materials.

Friends of Breckenridge Trails

Town of Breckenridge Open Space and Trails

PO Box 168, Breckenridge 80424; (970) 547-2251; www.townofbreckenridge.com

This group helps the Town of Breckenridge build and maintain trails in Breckenridge.

Friends of Dillon Ranger District

PO Box 1648, Silverthorne 80498-1648; (970) 262-3449; www.fdrd.org

FDRD helps the USDA Forest Service on various forest-related projects on national forest lands in Summit County.

This group focuses on trail maintenance and construction, conservation education, removing invasive weeds, and wild-land fire mitigation.

Friends of the Eagles Nest Wilderness

PO Box 4504, Frisco 80443-4504; www.fenw.org; or contact the Dillon Ranger District at (970) 468-5400 for the current contact

FENW helps the USDA Forest Service maintain trails and preserve wilderness values in the Eagles Nest, Holy Cross, and Ptarmigan Peak Wilderness Areas in Summit and Eagle Counties. Volunteer opportunities include trail projects, the Wilderness Volunteer program, invasive weed treatment, and fund-raising.

Volunteers for Outdoor Colorado

600 S. Marion Pkwy., Denver 80209; (303) 715-1010; www .voc.org

VOC is a nonprofit organization that sponsors work projects throughout Colorado, partnering with various land management agencies.

AMERICAN HIKING SOCIETY

Because you **hike.**

We're with you
every step of the way

American Hiking Society gives voice to the more than 75 million Americans who
hike and is the only national organization that promotes and protects foot trails,
the natural areas that surround them, and the hiking experience. Our work is
inspiring and challenging, and is built on three pillars:

Volunteerism and Stewardship

We organize and coordinate nationally recognized programs—including
Volunteer Vacations, National Trails Day ®, and the National Trails Fund—
that help keep our trails open, safe, and enjoyable.

Policy and Advocacy

We work with Congress and federal agencies to ensure funding for trails, the
preservation of natural areas, and the protection of the hiking experience.

Outreach and Education

We expand and support the national constituency of hikers through outreach
and education as well as partnerships with other recreation and conservation
organizations.

Join us in our efforts. Become an American Hiking Society member today!

**American
Hiking
Society**

1422 Fenwick Lane · Silver Spring, MD 20910 · (800) 972-8608
www.AmericanHiking.org · info@AmericanHiking.org